The Psychology of Ethics

*Understanding What It Takes
to Do the Right Thing
at the Right Time*

LOUIE V. LARIMER

ISBN: 978-0-9833123-0-7

Published By

Malama Pono Press
Colorado Springs, Colorado

This book is dedicated to the men and women of our armed forces. They endure personal hardships and risk their lives so that the expression of ideas in a free society can be maintained.

*Ethics begins with
understanding yourself, knowing
your psychology of ethics, and
making choices based upon
principles rather than situational
factors.*

CONTENTS

Preface

This book first came to life in 1997 under the title "Ethical Virtuosity: 7 Steps to Help You Discover and Do the Right Thing."

Many things have changed since that first manuscript was published. My knowledge of ethics has grown considerably. The word "terror" has taken on a new meaning for the people of the United States. We have experienced shifts in political and business leadership; seen changes in television, movie and media personalities; and benefited from advances in technology—all of which have contributed in some way to my discovery of new insights and different ways of knowing what it takes to do the right thing.

What has not changed since the first publication of this work is my strongly held conviction that it is not my place to define for you what is right or wrong.

Protagoras of Abdera is known to have said "When men differ, there is no single objective truth in virtue where one is right and the other is wrong."

Although other philosophers have disagreed with Protagoras, his subjective view of right and wrong provides support for my decision to refrain from declaring what is and is not ethical with respect to the most controversial issues of our time.

I leave such pronouncements to you and others. In my view, the right to decide right and wrong remains solely in your domain and prerogative.

This text therefore continues the original theme of Ethical Virtuosity which is that you have to figure out for yourself what is and is not ethical and you have to do the right thing at the right time—all on your own.

My purpose when I wrote Ethical Virtuosity was to provide knowledge, insight, frameworks, and principles for you to use in your ethical deliberations. My intent was to equip you to be able to decide for yourself what is the right thing to do in any situation you encounter. My purpose in writing this newly titled, updated edition remains the same.

I wrote this new edition in order to give you the benefit of my newly acquired knowledge of the psychology of ethics. Since 1997 when I wrote the first edition I have gained a greater understanding that discerning what is and is not ethical inherently involves a unique interplay of dynamic thoughts, ideas, beliefs, emotions, and personal memories. I have come to learn in a personal way that reason, passion, social pressures, social norms, law, history, world events, personal experiences, family influences, technological advances, mass media, spirituality, and religion all come into play as you try to figure out what is right and wrong in any situation.

Additionally, I have a better appreciation that the events of the external world impact the inner workings of the human mind. I have a greater understanding that the rational human mind conflicts with the emotional brain. I now have a deeper and more refined insight that sorting out, defining and doing the ethical thing is hard for many people. I have come to know that doing the right thing isn't easy to do in our faster paced and more complex world.

With its revised title, this new edition emphasizes the importance of understanding the inner workings of your mind in determining what is right and what is wrong. Hence, the shift from the concept of "Ethical Virtuosity" —being skilled and knowledgeable in resolving ethical dilemmas—to the concept of "The Psychology of Ethics" —understanding what it takes on the inside to be ethical —became a more appropriate organizing theme for the second edition.

Ethical Virtuosity—the notion of becoming a master at ethics—remains as a meaningful topic in this text. It is a helpful and relevant concept and it is a highly desirable goal for all of us.

The change in the title of the book, and the addition of new material is intended to help you to realize that there are many human psychological dynamics that come into play when you face ethical challenges. Knowing and mastering the inner workings of your psychology of ethics is fundamental to achieving Ethical Virtuosity.

The seven steps to Ethical Virtuosity described in the first edition remain unchanged in this revised text. The seven steps are fundamentally sound and lead to understanding and mastering the inner workings of the mind. As before, the seven steps will help you to discover and do the right thing at the right time.

I have included a new chapter on organizational ethics. Basically, it outlines twelve steps for organizational leaders to follow in developing an organizational ethics program. Organizations, as well as individuals, struggle with knowing and defining what is and is not ethical. The twelve steps leading to organizational ethical virtuosity will help organizational leaders figure out how to do the right thing at the right time.

Many people tell me that ethics or "doing the right thing" depends upon the circumstances or situational factors a person or organization faces at any given moment.

I struggle with the situational ethics approach because I have always believed that ethics should not depend on situations but upon the application of ethical principles. I have always believed you should base your decisions, particularly those involved with deciding what is right and wrong upon higher principles and concepts that you hold in high regard or value as being truly important to you.

I have always challenged those who believe that ethics depend upon the situation to identify for me the specific situational factor they believe is or should be the ultimate deciding factor of what is right and wrong. I ask those who adhere to the situational ethics philosophy to tell me how they know which situational factor, out of all of the multiple factors that may be present in a situation is the single most relevant factor upon which the right thing depends. In other words, I challenge people to identify for me the specific criteria they use to choose the situational factor in each dilemma they face. In essence, I want to know how a person determines the actual situational factor that is to take priority.

As expected, I am usually told, "Well, that depends!" The next several questions are "Why does it depend? And of course, "What does that dependent factor depend upon?"

The conversation then becomes a humorous exercise in circular thinking, and ultimately, an experience of realizing that the situational ethics advocates do not really know why or how they ultimately choose a particular factor or principle in any given ethical dilemma.

At this point in my Socratic exchange with the situational believers, I suggest, in an extremely polite way, that perhaps, those who say ethics depends upon the situation really do not have a pre-defined sense of ethics. Instead, they just "make up" or surreptitiously pick an ethical principle or situational factor to justify the inner "stirrings" within their minds concerning what is right and wrong. This statement usually produces various amusing facial expressions, including bewilderment, hesitation, realization, and on most occasions, curiosity.

As I further challenge folks to tell me the ethical principles or situational factors they rely upon when deciding right from wrong, something special begins to happen— people become more introspective as they respond to my challenge to identify and articulate ethical principles or situational factors.

It gets even more interesting when I challenge the situational ethicists to explain to me the psychological dynamics at work within their minds as they deliberate which situational factor is to take precedence in their determination of what is right and wrong.

Some people respond to my questioning by pausing, tuning into and becoming aware of what is happening inside of their minds. Other people become frustrated at what they consider to be my annoying and trivial questioning. Many people nod at me with an expression of insight realizing that there is a psychology of personal ethics operating within them that they are starting to recognize and understand.

As you read this latest edition, I hope you will learn more about your personal psychology of ethics. I hope you will be better prepared to discern right from wrong, and that you will choose ethical "principles" rather than situational factors as the foundation of your ethical beliefs.

Louie V. Larimer
January 2011

You have to figure out for yourself what is and is not ethical and you have to do the right thing at the right time —all on your own.

Acknowledgements

My appreciation and gratitude are warmly extended to the following people.

My wife, Grace, whose loving support and encouragement helped me complete this manuscript in a timely manner.

Aaron Brown, author, educator, and friend who knows the importance of the "substantive" dimension of leadership and is a strong supporter of my work in ethics.

John Anderson, psychologist and friend, who urged me to continue my efforts to develop meaningful and relevant ethics content during the beginning of my consulting career.

My high school teachers who saw something in me and urged me to go to college.

And most of all, to my parents whose patience, love, encouragement, and sacrifices made it possible for me to become more than I ever imagined possible.

Protagoras of Abdera is known to have said, "When men differ, there is no single objective truth in virtue where one is right and the other is wrong."

Part I

ETHICAL FOUNDATIONS

It isn't easy
to be an ethical person.

CHAPTER 1

The Ethics Challenge

Several years ago in January, a friend and I traveled to Phoenix, Arizona, to play golf, rest and enjoy the warm climate of Arizona for a few days. I had two round-trip airline tickets from Colorado Springs to Phoenix that were going to expire by the end of January if I did not use them. So I invited my friend, Dave, to join me. He eagerly agreed. We made some calls to Phoenix area resorts and found what we thought was a good golf package that included a double occupancy room, two rounds of golf, cart, range balls, free drinks and two free buffet breakfasts. We were quoted a figure that we thought was a bit pricey, but given our spontaneous desire to play golf and sit in the sun, we made reservations with the resort and were off to Phoenix the next day.

When Dave and I arrived at the resort, we signed in at the front desk, gave the clerk our credit cards, received the keys to our shared room, picked up our golf vouchers and eagerly awaited the arrival of the following morning so we could hit the course. We were like two children on

Christmas Eve, anxiously awaiting Santa's arrival.

To our disappointment, the next day turned out to be a rather cold, gray, windy day in Phoenix. Unfortunately, there was a frost delay and we had to wait several hours for the temperature to rise so that we could play. We kidded each other that we could have stayed in Colorado Springs and experienced the same weather for a lot less money! We eventually got on the course and played in conditions that were, to say the least, not very good.

Just before leaving, we asked the attendant what the normal green fees were for the course, in case we wanted to return someday without the resort's golf package. To our surprise, the green fees were pretty reasonable. As we drove back to the resort, we began to examine the "value" of our golf package, given the normal cost of the green fees and our estimation of the cost of our room.

Both Dave and I travel extensively for our businesses and are familiar with normal and customary hotel charges for business class, single occupancy accommodations. We both agreed that our double occupancy room fell below the standards to which we were accustomed as business travelers. The more we looked at the value of the golf package, the more we began to feel that it was not a great value. Rather, it seemed an exorbitant and unfair trade practice of the resort, particularly given the bad playing conditions we had experienced that day.

Rather than dwell on this negative feeling, we resigned ourselves to our situation. After all, no one forced us to go to Phoenix, and we both freely chose to accept the pricing when it was given to us over the phone. Since Dave and I are relatively upbeat, positive and optimistic people, we simply resolved that the next day's golf experience in the warmth and sun of the Arizona desert would more than offset the unsettled feelings of our first day.

Call it misfortune, destiny, fate or a cruel lesson in acceptance, we awoke the next morning to the exact same type of cold, gray, windy weather we had experienced the prior day. We were scheduled to play at a different golf course that required us to fight the congested morning traffic of metropolitan Phoenix. When we arrived at the course, there was no frost, but it was cold! We waited an hour, hoping for warmer weather. The sun taunted us by playing hide and seek in the clouds.

The morning finally got a little better and we played our second day of golf, once again, in conditions that were not what we had expected. After our round, we asked the attendant the regular price of a round of golf at the course. The green fee was almost double what had been quoted the day before. We felt a little better about our golf package given this new information.

However, our analytical business minds could not

resist repeating the examination and calculation of what we thought was our golf package's actual cost to the resort. Even with the higher green fees for that day, neither Dave nor I felt that we had received a genuine golf value, as had been promised to us by the resort over the phone.

Adding to our woes, Dave was suffering from the initial onset of the flu, and I had developed painful blisters on my left foot caused by a new pair of golf shoes. Further, it began to rain and neither of us felt like going out that night to experience the great dining pleasures Phoenix had to offer.

When we checked out the next morning, the clerk presented us with one bill, which seemed odd to me at the time since we had checked in separately. The price was exactly what I had been quoted on the phone. The only troubling aspect was that I had believed that the quoted price was a per person price, not a total price for two people. I was almost certain that I had clarified, at the time of making the reservation, that the quoted price was a per person price.

I thought that perhaps the clerk had made a mistake, but my reservations about the value of the golf package crept into my mind, and I was delighted that the final bill made our golf package a pretty good value. Still, I was troubled and felt that a mistake had been made by the clerk in our favor. But, I did not say anything at the time. Dave quickly gave the clerk his credit card and told her to put half of the charge on his card and the other half on mine. This she did without hesitation. We then went to enjoy our last free buffet breakfast before departing for the airport.

As we walked to the restaurant, we noticed that it was raining hard in Phoenix, the land of sun and desert. I felt uneasy and unsettled about the charges. Dave didn't feel the least bit concerned. He had not made the reservations, not been privy to my conversation with the reservation clerk, and he said we had gotten a great value after all, particularly given the weather we had endured. Still, during breakfast I was bothered that I had not spoken up and pointed out that the charge could not be right. I knew in my heart that if I had been overcharged, I would not have hesitated to point out the clerk's error. But for some reason, I had not spoken up when I was undercharged.

I mentioned all of this to Dave at breakfast and we discussed what I should do. He easily picked up on my discomfort and noted the irony in the situation, given that I am an ethics and compliance consultant.

Indeed, I was in the midst of a personal ethical dilemma. The more I recalled my conversation with the reservation clerk, the more strongly I felt that the final bill was wrong and that the checkout clerk had erred in our favor. If so, the correct bill, by our calculations, was exorbitant in light of the lower than business class accommodations we received, actual green fee charges and deplorable playing conditions.

During the remainder of our breakfast, I continued to be troubled by this incident and my own failure to press the issue with the checkout clerk. I couldn't help but recall a portion of an ethics speech I often deliver at conventions concerning personal choices. I was reminded of my observation that when you encounter or are confronted with an ethical dilemma, you have four choices.

The first is to ignore the dilemma and act or refrain from acting as if there was no ethical issue involved. This choice generally results in conduct that is unethical or unlawful. I had done this at the checkout counter and didn't feel good about that choice. Since we had not yet left the resort, I still had the opportunity to deal with the dilemma and make it right.

The second choice is to comply with the law or some other established ethical prescription, requirement or duty that specifically addresses the dilemma. This choice often results in what is considered by many to be ethical or honorable conduct. I gave this option some consideration and felt that I had not broken any law. I had simply paid the charges that had been presented to me by the clerk. I did feel that perhaps under contract principles of law, I had made a legally enforceable promise to pay at the per person quoted price. But then again, hadn't the resort waived the per-person price when it presented its final bill, which we paid? The option of following the law or fulfilling some prescribed duty wasn't of great solace to me.

The third choice is to consciously disregard the law, as well as any applicable code of conduct, and act in an unlawful or unethical manner. Since the law didn't really apply to my dilemma on this particular day, this choice was not an option for me and my beliefs.

The fourth choice I have often urged others to consider is to act in a manner that exceeds the minimum requirements of the law and to engage in a more noble and virtuous course of action that reflects ethics, integrity and responsible personal conduct. I was bothered that I had not done this at the time of checkout, but I still had time to go back and revisit the issue with the clerk.

As I finished my breakfast and discussed these options with Dave, I knew that I still had to make a choice. I really had two options. The first was to take advantage of what I believed was the clerk's error by ignoring the dilemma and rationalizing the mistake as some form of ethical justice in light of our perceptions that we had not received a good golf value. The second choice was for me to return to the front desk and bring my concerns to the clerk's attention.

I was really struggling with this issue and not totally settled upon a course of action, when the checkout clerk appeared at our table explaining that she had made a mistake on our final bill. She asked if we would come to the front desk to rerun our credit cards to add the charges she had missed. She explained that they had lost one of the reservations and the bill she gave us at our checkout was for a party of one, not two.

I was actually relieved that my dilemma had been resolved. Now I didn't have to make a choice. I didn't have to confront my inner feelings, weaknesses and vulnerabilities. My dilemma was over. We paid the revised final bill without complaint. We made no mention of our feelings of disappointment. After all, we did have a choice whether or not to come to Phoenix after being quoted the price.

As I've reflected upon my Phoenix golf experience, I have felt regret and disappointment in myself. I now know that I should have acted upon my ethical instincts that something was wrong during the checkout. I should have pursued the matter at the time the clerk gave me the bill, rather than agonizing over it during breakfast. In retrospect, I like to think that I would not have left the resort without having the clerk recheck our bill to make sure she had not made an error in our favor. At least that's what I hope I would have done!

A Learning Experience

I learned a few things from this experience. I'm grateful for the opportunity it gave me to gain greater insight into myself. I've even made a few observations about how hard it is to do the right thing.

For example, the choice you make in any given ethical dilemma is a function of your: personality, moral character, inner strength, personal core values, internal sense of what is right and wrong, moral courage, integrity, honor and ethical fitness.

These qualities are the result of several competing influences, such as your: family, peers, friends, education, religious beliefs, culture, worldly experiences, the media and even unconscious motivations and influences.

The competing nature of these varied influences frequently makes choosing and following the right ethical and moral path a difficult task.

Additionally, there are numerous temptations (e.g., ego, greed, lust, power, sex, etc.) and inner personal conflicts (e.g., self-interest versus concern for others, peer pressure versus individuality, truth versus loyalty, mercy versus justice, and conscious versus unconscious drives) that get in the way of doing the right thing.

In some cases, doing the right thing requires self-sacrifice for the betterment of others. In other cases, it requires taking an unpopular stand that subjects you to the criticism of others. Sometimes, the right or ethical thing to do is not even readily apparent to you. And in some situations, doing the right thing might be harmful to others who may be innocent bystanders.

The emotional context or circumstances of a dilemma often cause you to be unable to accurately perceive and discern the true, ethical, or moral path. In some dilemmas, you are forced by circumstances beyond your control to choose between the lesser of two evils, thereby making the choice a painful and hurtful one. There are even occasions when you must choose between what appears to you to be two rights.

Indeed, doing the right thing is not as easy as simply talking or writing about it. Let's face it: doing the right thing often requires a lot from us as human beings.

Unlike many scholars, philosophers and professional ethicists, I don't profess to know what is right and wrong, nor do I have any particularly meaningful insights as to the ultimate moral principles by which you should live your life, or conduct your business.

Over the course of my life, I have learned that there are certain rules or principles of living which I believe if followed, lead to a happier, meaningful, and more abundant life. (See *Don't Poke the Gorilla in the Eye! 50 Rules for Insightful Living* (2010) by Louie V. Larimer.)

I have also learned from my personal experiences and reflections, that ethics, integrity, responsible personal conduct, and honor are important concepts to know, understand, appreciate, and to incorporate into one's daily behavior.

Many great philosophers have observed that a person's ethics are revealed and demonstrated by personal behavior and private conduct. In other words, what you do—how you respond to the events and challenges in your life—reveal your ethical makeup. I believe this to be true. If you want to know more about your ethical constitution, or want to know the ethics of another person, pay less attention to what you and others say, but look closely at what you and others do. Behaviors reflect choices that are driven by your ethics.

I also believe that ethics, integrity and responsible personal conduct can be taught. I believe that people can, under the right circumstances, change their attitudes, beliefs, and behavior patterns and live more virtuous, caring and loving lives.

At a personal level, this kind of change requires that you make a formal commitment to reflect and demonstrate ethics, integrity and responsible personal conduct in all that you do. Specifically, this commitment requires that you consistently resolve ethical or moral dilemmas in a manner that reflects goodness and virtue. This concept is what I call "Ethical Virtuosity."

Ethical Virtuosity is developed or acquired by regularly engaging in and practicing seven specific steps: becoming self-aware, seeking ethical knowledge, developing an ethical belief system, practicing emotional discipline, consciously exercising your free will, demonstrating moral courage and personal accountability, and most important, immediately acting on your personal commitment to become ethically virtuous. These seven steps are explained further in Part II of this book.

At an organizational level, Ethical Virtuosity can be developed by a genuine institutional commitment by an organization's top leaders to follow twelve easy steps or strategies. These steps are outlined in Part III. If these strategies are implemented by an organization's leaders, a highly ethical organization can be built and maintained.

The underlying purposes of this book are to help you: make ethical decisions in your personal and professional life; better understand the psychology and nature of your personal ethics; identify, articulate and defend the criteria, principles, standards and values that comprise your ethical belief system; and lastly, inspire you and other organizational leaders to make ethics, integrity, and personal accountability a greater priority in your daily work.

I hope to fulfill these purposes by introducing you to some notable moral philosophies and ethical principles; explaining the nature of certain moral qualities or virtues; offering you a few of my personal insights; sharing with you several ethical tools and analytical processes; making inquiries of you about your moral personality and ethical preferences; asking you to identify your core ethical values, moral beliefs, and ethical principles; asking you tough controversial questions; presenting you with a variety of ethical scenarios and asking you to determine the right thing to do.

If you listen to your inner dialogue, if you are mindful of your thoughts and feelings during this process, you will learn a few things about yourself and your psychology of ethics.

My Perspective

I offer my observations with a certain degree of trepidation. My concerns include the following:

- What do I really know about ethics, integrity, character, psychology, responsible personal conduct, and honor?
- What qualifies me to write about these matters?
- Am I any more ethical than my friends, colleagues, business associates and competitors?

- What will others think about me after reading this work?
- Will people think I am a hypocrite, recalling past experiences when they may have thought I acted unethically?
- Am I just setting myself up for criticism by taking on this project?

I feel compelled to disclose to you that when I first wrote this book I was a practicing lawyer. I know that for some of you, this automatically disqualifies me from having any credibility and knowledge of ethics. And yet, my experiences as a lawyer have given me the opportunity to see, experience, and deal in a practical manner with the consequences of unethical decisions and conduct.

Don't you think that most, if not all, lawsuits originate because someone does not act in accordance with the ethical principles of honesty, integrity, and personal accountability?

Even so, what qualifies me to write about the psychology of ethics and Ethical Virtuosity? Just because I've seen the devastating results of unethical conduct does not necessarily mean I am capable of providing you with any meaningful ethical insights. I ask your indulgence and your openness before rendering judgment.

I am the product of a traditional liberal arts education. Because of that I have probably spent a bit more time than the average business executive thinking about abstract and esoteric notions of classical human thought and human experience. After all, what else can you do with a liberal arts education?

I attended a Jesuit graduate business school and took useful and practical courses such Business and Society, Corporate Social Responsibility, and Business Policy. My fellow MBA students referred to these courses as soft, nontechnical electives. I referred to them as "lifesavers," since they were the only graduate courses I could really understand. I still struggle with the principles of ratio analysis and internal rates of return!

Given this educational background, I had no choice but to either teach or become a lawyer. I chose the safe, conservative route and did both! I convinced a few academic vice presidents that I could handle the rigors of teaching the required business ethics course, as well as the mandatory course on business law. Hence, I've been privileged to teach ethics, law, leadership, and conflict resolution at several graduate business schools. I have also been given the opportunity to present ethics talks at many national conferences and leadership institutes, I have also been privileged to conduct ethics courses for both corporate entities and government organizations.

In order to teach these courses, I was forced to read a great volume of literature pertaining to business, government, and professional ethics, as well as, a fair amount of history and philosophy. As any good college professor knows, you have to stay at least one chapter ahead of your class. There is always one eager beaver who's out to test your knowledge!

And so, it is from this pragmatic and slightly scholastic perspective that I offer you my insights on the psychology of ethics and the concept of ethical virtuosity.

What is Inside

Here is a sampling of the questions, topics, and issues that are addressed in the pages that follow:

- What is ethics?
- What is law?
- How does law differ from ethics?
- What is integrity?
- What is character?
- Why are ethics, integrity, and character important?
- What is ethical virtuosity?
- Where do ethical and moral beliefs originate and how do they evolve?
- Why do people act unethically?
- What ethical principles do people actually use when confronted with moral or ethical dilemmas?

- What is a core ethical value?
- Why are core values important?
- What is emotional discipline?
- What is reflective judgment?
- What is free will?
- What is moral courage?
- How does one overcome temptation and the problem of human fallibility?
- How does a leader promote, inspire and encourage ethical virtuosity in an organization?

Before going further, I want to challenge you at a personal level. Specifically, I want to provoke a few thoughts and feelings within you. I urge you to be mindful of your reactions and search for the meaning stirring within you.

Here are a few questions that only you can answer:

- Are you one of those executives who pay lip service to the principles of ethics, integrity, character, personal accountability and honor?
- Is your behavior and conduct consistent with your ethical talk?
- Do you truly have, and genuinely know, your own ethical standards and values?
- Have you acted in a questionable or unethical manner lately?
- Why did you do so?
- What, if anything, did you learn about yourself from that experience?

- Are you aware of any unethical, unlawful, or questionable conduct in your organization?

- What, if anything, did you do about it?

- Do you even care?

- How do you respond to a known ethical violation by a superior? By a subordinate? By a close friend or colleague?

- What do you think these responses reveal about your ethical constitution?

- Do you truly know what principles guide your decisions and behavior when confronted by an ethical dilemma?

- Can you look at your own conduct and articulate the internal principles that shaped your behavior in a given circumstance?

- Are you willing to honestly look at yourself from an ethical perspective?

- Do you know your core ethical values?

I encourage you to honestly reflect upon these questions before reading further. Your answers to these questions will provide valuable insight into your own ethical constitution and give you a foundation for incorporating the concepts that are presented in the following chapters.

Finally, I want to emphasize that I offer my observations simply as a means of helping you discover for yourself certain ethical truths, knowledge, and insights that I believe you have buried deep within your soul, conscience, and heart. It is not my intention to teach you absolute universal principles of ethics. You must discover them yourself.

It is my most sincere intention, however, to help you discover or reconnect with your ethical beliefs by getting you to undertake a deliberate journey inward.

This book is intended to be a catalyst in your personal, continuing quest for self-discovery, self-exploration, self-mastery, and ethical achievement.

If you move in this direction, I guarantee that you will find many new insights and substantial personal rewards. As is the case with any personal journey inward, the extent to which you benefit is totally up to you. To paraphrase Galileo, you cannot teach someone about worldly wisdom, at best, you can only help them to discover it within his or her self.

*Ethics doesn't have
to be abstract, esoteric
or complex.*

CHAPTER 2

What Is Ethics?

I begin every ethics talk or seminar in the same way. As a person of Hawaiian descent, I speak a few simple phrases of Hawaiian to the audience, and then I introduce the participants to two Hawaiian words.

The first word is "kapu." It means that which is prohibited, forbidden, or off limits. Kapu is known as the collection of principles which governed all relationships in the world of the *ka po'e kahiko*—the ancient people of old Hawaii.

Among other things, kapu defined the nature of the relationship between the ruling class of people, the *ali'i*, and the *maka ainana*, the common people of the islands.

The people of old Hawaii believed that the ali'i were embodied with *mana*—a divine spiritual power or presence that could be lost if certain rituals and customs were not followed. Kapu set forth those rituals which the common people were to follow in order to maintain the mana of the ali'i.

The Hawaiian people also believed that kapu was intended to promote *lokahi*—harmony between the commoners and the ali'i. For the ancient Hawaiians, kapu established what could and could not be done by the maka ainana and the ali'i.

The kapu principles were very strict. Enforcement was rigid, and violations of kapu resulted in severe consequences, generally death.

Kapu was the ideological system of rights, privileges, and prohibitions that when followed by all Hawaiians maintained a sense of order and balance between the people and the royalty.

In the Western world, kapu is akin to the concept of the social contract theory which was said to govern the relationship between people and government.

Under the social contract theory, people were entitled to certain rights such as life, liberty, and happiness. These rights were granted in exchange for the performance of certain duties that were owed to the ruling authority, such as the payment of taxes. In some cases, the ruling authority was a reigning monarch. In other cases, it was an emerging democratic form of government.

The ruling authority, limited in its powers, and had certain responsibilities such as providing for the common defense of the people. In the United States, the social contract between the citizens and the government is embodied in the United States Constitution and its Amendments.

One of earliest written social contracts in the Western world is the magna carta which limited the powers of King John of England in 1215. In this early writing, King John proclaimed the existence of certain personal liberties and acknowledged that his powers could not be arbitrarily exercised.

In the Hawaiian world, kapu not only governed the relationship between the people and the ali'i, but it also set forth the customs that were to be followed by the people in their interactions with each other. Kapu defined what the people could and could not do with *aina* (land) and *moana* (ocean)—serving as the first environmental protections for Hawaiian ecosystems.

Kapu also dictated how the Hawaiian people were to behave with respect to the spirit world and their pantheistic conceptions of the Hawaiian gods. The Hawaiian people believed there was Ke Akua (Great God) and thousands of other minor gods; the most popular of which were Kane, Lono, Ku, and Pele. Hawaiian scholars estimate that there are over 400,000 minor gods in the Hawaiian spirit world. See, Kanahele, G., Ku Kanaka (University of Hawaii Press 1986).

Under the Kapu system, spiritual rituals were mandated which were intended to appease the gods and keep harmony with the spirits of Hawaii.

Lastly, Kapu provided the Hawaiian people with customs, rituals, and principles they were expected to follow in order to maintain a healthy, wholesome, and balanced relationship with the individual "self" consisting of mind, body, and spirit.

In essence, Kapu governed every aspect of Hawaiian life and defined what was right and wrong conduct.

The second Hawaiian concept I introduce to every participant in my ethics sessions is the word "pono." It means that which is righteous and just. Pono is the word for those ideas, practices, behaviors, rituals and customs which were considered to be right. Knowing and doing the "right thing" was a strong and fundamental precept for the people of old Hawaii.

Even today, the official state motto of Hawaii bears this cultural notion of doing that which is right. Proclaimed by Kamehameha III on July 31, 1843 following a brief military takeover of Honolulu by Lord Paulet of the Royal Navy of Great Britain, the phrase:*"Ua mau ke ea o ka aina i ka pono"* became deeply imbedded within the heart of every person of Hawaiian ancestry and was adopted as the state's motto in 1959.

The phrase translated into English means: "The life of the land is perpetuated by righteousness."

In essence, kapu and pono are the Hawaiian equivalents of our modern day philosophical and pragmatic notions of ethics and of the right thing to do.

In its most simplistic definition, ethics refers to the principles of right and wrong. Ethics is the body of knowledge that defines morality in our current world. Like kapu, ethics governs, influences and shapes our relationships with our government, each other, our physical environment, our spirituality, and our individual components of self.

The Nature of Ethics

Do you have ethics? Do you have a set of consciously chosen, deliberately developed principles or values you use to resolve the ethical dilemmas that occur in your life? Do you have specific criteria that define what is and is not ethical? Like the Hawaiians of old, do you know what kapu requires of you? Do you know what pono is?

When I ask these questions during my ethics presentations, everyone in the audience raises their hands and nods affirmatively indicating that they have ethics.

When I ask if anyone in the audience has attended an ethics training session at work, or has had an ethics class in school, almost all of the participants' hands go up indicating a positive response to my question.

When this happens, I show a concerned look on my face and remark to the audience that I am in serious trouble. Since everyone in the room has ethics, everyone must be an expert in his or her own psychology of ethics. I woefully remark that since everyone has a clear notion of ethics, what could I possibly contribute to their ethical knowledge? I ask in a playful and apologetic manner: "What could I possibly say to them that they did not already know?" " Furthermore, what in the world was I going to talk about for four hours that could make any difference since everyone already had ethics?"

Think for a moment about your reaction to my questions. Don't you have ethics? Don't you know the difference between right and wrong? Don't you have a set of principles, values and guidelines that define what is right from wrong? Wouldn't you raise your hand in response to my question of who has ethics?

Let me ask you a few direct and personal questions. The answers are easy and I know you be going to be able to answer without hesitation.

Do you have a pet? If so, can you tell me the following things about your pet? What is your pet's name? What color is your pet? What kind of breed is your pet? How would you describe your pet's personality? How much does your pet weigh?

Do you have a car? What is the make and model of your car? How old is your car? How many miles has your car been driven? What color is the outside of the car?

What is the color of the interior? Does it have an automatic or standard transmission? How well does it run?

How about a house or an apartment? Do you have a dwelling place? How big is it? How many rooms does it have? What color is it on the outside? Does it have a garage? How many cars will the garage accommodate? Can you describe what the kitchen looks like? When did you buy or get your house or apartment?

Pretty easy questions weren't they? Well, how about I ask the same kinds of questions again, but this time, since you said you have ethics, let me ask questions about your personal ethics.

How many ethics do you have? What are your ethics? What is your definition of an ethical act? What is the central theme of your ethics? Where do you keep your ethics? Can you show me your ethics? Do you have them with you right now? What is the foundation of your ethics? What criteria do you use in deciding right from wrong? When did you get your ethics? How do you really know the difference between right and wrong?

If you are like my ethics class participants, the answers to these questions are not as quick and forth coming as the answers to my prior questions about pets, cars and houses.

If you are like most people in my ethics classes, when I asked you about your ethics, you paused, hesitated, and searched for something meaningful to say rather than give a glib or superficial answer.

The difference in the response to the ethics questions results from the fact that the nature of ethics is abstract and intangible. There is no physical substance to describe and the answers to the questions about your personal ethics require more reflection and searching to find than the answers to the questions about your pet, car or house.

Ethics is inherently esoteric. Ethical principles are abstract. You cannot directly see your ethics. Ethics consists of thoughts, ideas, beliefs, and concepts. Furthermore, most of us have never had the desire, interest, opportunity or time to actually reflect upon the nature of our ethical beliefs and our psychology of ethics.

What I have discovered from teaching ethics over the span of twenty-five years is that people will tell me they have ethics, but when pressed by me for greater information about the nature of their personal ethics, most people have a very difficult time being able to readily identify, articulate, and defend their ethics.

How about you? Looking honestly at your responses to my questions about your ethics, do you truly know the nature of your ethics? Do you know the dynamics of your ethical thinking? Do you know your psychology of ethics? What criteria do you use to determine what is right from wrong? What is your definition of an ethical act?

Consider for a moment that your favorite grandchild, son or daughter, niece or nephew, brother or sister, or some other close personal friend comes to you and tells you that he is in the midst of an ethical crisis. He says that he genuinely does not know what to do. He relates that he is torn between several conflicting interests and feelings.

Assume that this special person also asks for your insight as to how he ought to go about resolving the dilemma. He tells you he doesn't want you to tell him what to do, nor does he want you to tell him specifically what you think is right or wrong. He asks simply for your insight as to what "ethics" would require of him in his analysis and decision. He asks you to explain to him the meaning of "ethics."

Would you be able to offer meaningful and helpful insights? What would you say? How would you respond to your child?

Does the word "ethics" have a special meaning for you? Can you define it in a way that is simple, understandable and meaningful so that even a young child could comprehend it? Do you know, at a personal level, what ethics really requires of you as a person?

A Beginning Definition

According to most dictionaries, ethics refers to generally accepted principles, judgments, or notions of what is right and wrong, good and evil, moral and immoral. The word is derived from the Greek "ethos" meaning custom, practice or usage.

Many people use the word ethics interchangeably with "moral." In fact, several dictionaries list "moral," as a secondary definition for "ethics."

Philosophers and scholars use the word "ethics" to refer to the systematic, disciplined study of or inquiry into what is right and wrong and in some cases, what ought to be considered as right or wrong. For these individuals, "ethics" is an organized compilation of judgments, principles and concepts that define what is right and wrong, and tell us how we ought to live our lives.

Six Levels of Ethics

There are six levels at which ethics can be discussed: personal, cultural, societal, professional, generational, and organizational.

Personal Ethics

Personal ethics are those judgments of right and wrong made by an individual. They consist of certain principles, values and duties that a person believes ought to be the basis for personal conduct. Personal ethics are seldom, if ever, embodied in written form. They exist within your soul, your conscience and your heart. They are reflected in your daily decisions, life choices and personal conduct.

Personal ethics vary considerably from person to person. A person who violates his personal code of ethics can, if he has a conscience or a personal sense of integrity, suffer anxiety, guilt, or remorse.

Aristotle tells us that a person's ethics are revealed not by one's speech, talk, or rhetoric, but rather by what one does on a daily basis and how one behaves. Buddha tells us that a person's true ethics are exposed during times of personal crisis—when one's surroundings, circumstances and environment have become hostile or are no longer comfortable.

As I mentioned above, many people innocently, but mistakenly, believe that they possess a well-thought-out, formal and personal code of ethics.

In my work, I often ask people to identify, articulate and defend the ethical principles, values and beliefs that govern, dictate, or influence their lives. Most people, when confronted with such an inquiry, generally pause, become somewhat reflective and then offer a few superficial, abstract and popular pronouncements which they believe constitute their ethical belief system.

In reality, most people have not taken the time to consciously identify, contemplate and choose their guiding ethical principles.

Despite this experience, I do believe that every person possesses a unique ethical belief system. At times, the underlying principles, values and beliefs may not be readily or consciously apparent, resulting in personal conduct that lacks a clear articulated basis. In other words, many personal ethical belief systems exist at an unconscious level, thereby resulting in choices and conduct that have no originating conscious foundation.

Cultural Ethics

Cultural ethics are those notions of right and wrong that are embraced by a particular ethnic or cultural group. These notions of right and wrong are seldom written, but exist in the minds and hearts of people who share a common cultural bond. The violation of a cultural ethic generally results in a judgment of disfavor or ostracism by the group against the individual who violated the cultural ethical norm.

I grew up in Hawaii, a genuine, cosmopolitan melting pot of cultural diversity. I witnessed and experienced the clash of cultural ethics almost daily as I lived within this unique island smorgasbord of culture. The following ethnic groups have a strong and vibrant presence in Hawaii: Native Hawaiians, other Pacific Islanders, Caucasians, Japanese, Chinese, Filipino and Portuguese. Each of these ethnic groups have distinctive views of what is right and wrong.

For example, the Hawaiian culture places a great value

on love, openness, easy living, free spiritedness, pleasure and happiness. Time is of little importance to most ethnic Hawaiians. There is a principle in Hawaii known as "Hawaiian Time." It refers to the notion that Hawaiians will often appear at an engagement, whether for work, a business meeting, or a luncheon date, at a time that may or may not coincide with the agreed upon scheduled time. I often jokingly remarked to my Caucasian and Asian friends that the only time Hawaiians were ever on time was for a luau, party, or some other festive activity, provided the event didn't interfere with whatever was going on at the moment!

The free spiritedness of the Hawaiians, and the cultural value placed on easy living, is in direct contrast with the Asian cultural notions of industriousness, attention to detail, hard work, promptness and duty over pleasure. As you might imagine, these cultural notions of right and wrong often resulted in the members of each culture feeling the other culture was wrong with respect to the importance of time, work and other aspects of life.

Most people in the United States have a significant cultural or ethnic bond. For example, each of us probably characterizes ourselves as being a member of, or heavily influenced by, one of the many cultural groups that migrated into the United States. Whether it is Italian, German, French, English, Scandinavian, African,

Spanish, Arab, Jew, or Asian, each culture possesses a unique ethical belief system of what is right and wrong. As a member of a cultural or ethnic group, you are undoubtedly influenced in some way by distinctive cultural ethics.

In the movie, *My Big Fat Greek Wedding*, the main character a young Greek woman named Toola falls in love with a man who is not Greek. Initially, her family is shocked since her culture expects her to marry a Greek man. The movie portrays in a humorous manner the many cultural differences and cultural quirks the families of the bride and groom encounter.

In one of my favorite scenes, as Toola walks down the church aisle with her disappointed and reluctant to give her away father, we see her Greek family members and friends "spitting" at her as she passes by them. She smiles and nods at each one while the groom's parents are horrified at this barbaric and outlandish behavior. It is later on in the movie that we learn the 'spitting" is actually a gesture of good-will intended to shoo away the bad spirits which may adversely affect Toola's wedding day and marriage.

Each of one of us is a member of a culture. Each one of us has a unique cultural bond which at some level influences our choices and behaviors when we encounter an ethical dilemma.

When we travel abroad and visit other cultures, the differing customs and rituals may seem odd to us. Likewise, our own cultural notions seem odd to those from other cultures. I am reminded of the rule often uttered by some who travel abroad; "When in Rome, do as the Romans do."

If you are a member of a cultural group, like Toola in the movie, you too have been subjected to overt, and at times, very subtle pressures to comply with cultural norms. Like Toola, failure to comply with these cultural ethics can result in emotional conflict, cultural scorn and ostracism.

Societal Ethics

Societal ethics are those judgments of right and wrong possessed by a distinctive society. Societal ethics are unwritten. They are similar to cultural ethics, but apply to a grouping of people that include many diverse cultures.

When cultures come together and settle in geographical areas in close proximity, mixing of cultural values ethics and notions of right and wrong occur. When cultures begin to share common notions of right and wrong, societal ethics emerge. Societal ethics are best understood, perhaps, by thinking of working classes, economic factors, and geographical regions with cultural or ethnic characteristics distributed throughout those distinctions.

In most communities in America, there are still clear cut, highly identifiable and visible societal groupings. Those who belong to prestigious, exclusive membership organizations such as country or golf clubs tend to hold notions of right and wrong behavior that differ greatly from other clubs and associations that are less restrictive and more inclusive.

For example, I was raised in a working class family and I associated with other similarly situated families, without the benefit of prestigious country clubs and "high class" events, such as debutante balls, the symphony and the ballet. I remember participating in and enjoying numerous social events and activities that most members of my current golf club would probably frown at or look upon with dismay. As result of my early socialization, today I prefer, without hesitation, a good, boisterous, friendly, down to earth, barbecue at a local park, followed by a visit to a carnival, over that of the formality, elegance and quiet beauty of the symphony or ballet.

I do not intend by these observations to promote societal or class differences and stereotypes, rather, I make these observations to illustrate that such differences still exist at a societal level and that they affect societal ethics.

Just as with the violation of a cultural ethical principle,

the violation of a societal ethic generally results in social condemnation.

I have visited many parts of the United States and have encountered many differing societal norms. For example, in New York and other east coast cities, the people seem much different to me than the people in Hawaii. To me, those on the east coast, regardless of their ethnic background seem to be always in a rush, hurried, a bit opinionated, and more than willing to share their opinions even when unsolicited. Many people in New York appear to me to be abrupt, brash, cold, focused, time oriented, and somewhat rude. I know this is not the case with all who live in New York or the east coast, but ... they are different than the easy going, happy, friendly, and slow moving people of Hawaii!

During one of my visits to New York City, my wife Grace and I had our first experience with a New York cab driver who terrified Grace with his aggressive driving tactics which included incessant horn blowing, sudden accelerations, quick stops, unexpected lane changes, friendly and "unfriendly" gestures to other drivers and pedestrians, not to mention a metaphorically rich, graphic, and colorful vocabulary which he used to motivate others who crossed his path in undesirable ways.

Hawaii does not have cab drivers like the one we encountered in New York. When I told others about our cabbie, those more experienced with the New York scene told me that our experience was not unusual and that was just the way it was in that part of the country.

During the same trip, I visited a New York delicatessen and I ordered a pastrami sandwich on white bread, with mayonnaise and cheddar cheese. I was mortified when I was publicly ridiculed and forthrightly admonished by the proprietor and other diners who had heard my order. Apparently, as everyone in New York knows, you never put pastrami on white bread with mayo. The societal norm is pastrami on rye with mustard! The shame and humiliation I experienced as I was scorned by all in the restaurant was enough to clearly embed in my mind how to correctly order a pastrami sandwich in New York City.

In the southern part of the United States, there is a Southern way of living and treating others. Regardless of their cultural background, people in the south wave to you as you drive along their back country roads. They seem cordial, neighborly, pleasant, and have an appealing niceness about themselves. At least that has been my experience during my trips.

During one of my visits to the south, I observed that southern folks also have a rather unique way of being able to talk bad about other people—sometimes even in the presence of the person they are talking about. Apparently, in the south, this custom is acceptable and practiced regularly by many people, regardless of ethnicity. In the south, talking about others, even in an unkindly manner is not looked upon with disfavor as long as you preface your comments with the magic words: "Bless his heart ... or Bless your heart."

Trust me, if you hear these words while you are in the south you can bank on it that what follows will be gossip about another person, or a derogatory comment. As incredible as it may seem, the words that follow even though derogatory will sound so nice and have an acceptable ring to you!

The people who live in and around New Orleans are a unique mixture of ethnic backgrounds reflecting an eclectic combination of French, Spanish, American Indian, Caribbean, African, and English people. The food, customs, way of life, attitudes, philosophies, and spirituality are all blended in a way that give the people of New Orleans a distinctive society popularized by their mardi gras celebrations each year.

This annual event crosses and touches all aspects of the New Orleans region. There is sensuality, a connection with life, a raw humanness, an excitement, an edginess, and a closeness to the spirit world which is prevalent across all ethnic groups. In New Orleans there is a way of life, a way of doing things, an attitude of what is and what is not right conduct. One of my favorite things about New Orleans is the saying: "laissez bon temps roulette" which means—let the good times roll.

In New Orleans they even have their own slang which is shared across cultures and is therefore a societal ethic. For example, if you order a roast beef sandwich in New Orleans you will be asked if you want "debris" with that sandwich. This means do want to have the small pieces of the roast beef which have fallen off into the pot and float in the juices. Or, you might be asked when you order a hamburger whether you want that "dressed" meaning do you want that served with lettuce, tomato, and mayonnaise.

Hawaii provides numerous examples of societal ethics shared by the many cultures that live in the Islands. Did you know that in Hawaii it is customary that you remove your shoes when entering a person's home? Did you know that rice is the preferred breakfast side dish with eggs rather than potatoes? Did you know that Spam is a preferred breakfast meat option at most local Hawaiian diners? Again, these are not notions of right and wrong that are of a single culture, but are cross-cultural and therefore have become societal ethics.

We have many societies in the United States, and we have many differing notions of what is right and wrong personal conduct in those societies. There is a saying: "When in Rome, do as the Romans do." This cryptic piece of advice recognizes the profound influence of societal ethics, norms and customs which bring pressure to conform and act in accordance with those principles of right and wrong within those societies.

Professional Ethics

Professional ethics are those standards of conduct required of those who are members of a particular profession, trade, or occupation, such as medicine, law, engineering, or accounting. These ethical standards of conduct have been developed by the profession and are regarded as the minimum expected behavior from members of the profession. These standards are written, codified and widely distributed among members of the profession. In essence, these professional ethics define the expected and acceptable behavior for the profession. Violating a professional ethic results in some form of professional discipline, including, but not limited to, admonition, probation, suspension, or expulsion from the professional group.

Today, almost every professional, trade and occupational association has developed some form of professional code of ethics that governs its members. Do a quick internet search of your profession and add to the search parameters the key words "code of conduct or ethics." You will find many references to what is acceptable conduct as a member of your profession.

Generational Ethics

Generational Ethics refers to the notions of right and wrong shared by people of a specific generation who lived and experienced common events and times that shaped their thoughts and beliefs of what is right and how to live your life.

Much has been written about The Greatest Generation, the Baby Boomers, Gen Xers, Generation Y and the Millenniums, etc. The writings about these generations, and our interactions with them confirm that there are great differences in how each generation thinks and behaves.

In my parents' generation, the word divorce was not uttered in polite society. In their time, you married for life regardless of whether or not a person changed. In my generation, divorce is common. My parents' generation would never have even thought of living with someone without being married. In my generation that trend emerged, and with the generation of my children it is most common.

In my adolescence, I "dated" and went "steady" with my high school sweet heart. When I asked a girl out on a date, I went to her house, picked her up, went out, paid for everything, and brought her home at curfew.

Today, my children, don't date or go steady, they do something called "hook-up." I asked my children what that meant, and they smiled, laughed at me and uttered "You don't really want to know Dad." I recently find out that in my children's generation, a boy does not even have to call a girl to hook up. All a young man needs to do is meet a young woman on something called "Facebook" and then they go "hang" together for a while.

A few years back, I was teaching ethics to a group of seasoned, tough minded, older police sergeants of a major metropolitan police department. The group was bemoaning their perceived loss of work ethic and professionalism among newer generation police rookies coming out of the police academy. One robust sergeant told me the story of a Generation X rookie who mouthed off to him during the rookie's first day on the force. He explained with a very subtle smile, but with a noticeable look of confusion how he had reacted too quickly, and "taught" the recruit some "ethics" by taking him into the back room and "knocking" some sense into the rookie.

When I asked him to explain further, he told me his generation of officers would have never lipped off to a sergeant, that was what they were taught, that was the way it was, and that is how it ought to be regardless of your generation.

I asked him with a smile if his tactic with the rookie was an effective strategy and if he would do it again if the same or similar situation arose. He told me his tactic certainly seemed highly effective at the time, and even in the days that followed he believed he had done the right thing. He went on to tell me that he subsequently got an advisory letter from the police chief to refrain from teaching "ethics" to the rookies and that he was to leave the teaching of ethics to the department's newly retained ethics consultant!

Organizational Ethics

Organizational ethics are those standards of behavior expected of persons who work for an organization. They take many forms. You will find them reflected in value statements, organizational policies and employee codes of conduct. In many organizations, the organizational ethics are unwritten, but can be discerned from the behavior of the top leadership. Violating an organizational ethic can result in ostracism and discipline.

Just as with personal ethics, organizational ethics vary considerably from organization to organization. Some organizations operate with little sense of business responsibility without regard for how their conduct might affect others. Other organizations are highly ethical, demanding that the business conduct of their employees promote and exemplify certain highly regarded and noble virtues.

Enron's organizational ethics, centered on a culture of self interest, deception, and improper financial and accounting practices eventually led to its demise. The organizational ethics of Bernard Madoff's investment firm were grounded on making false representations to potential investors and "cooking" the books in order to hide the theft of investor funds and make it appear that investor money was yielding high returns. Crime enterprises and inner city gangs are held together by organizational principles, values, and ethics which are well known within these groups and rigidly enforced.

On a positive note, there are many organizations that are founded on more virtuous ethical principles that inspire attitudes, decisions and personal behavior resulting in ethical behavior. We do not often hear about these organizations and their practices since the media does not focus on them and it is an ethical norm within these organizations to be humble and refrain from self promotion of their virtuous conduct.

Organizational ethics reflect the personal ethics and values of its leaders and managers. That is why focusing on and understanding your personal ethics is so important in your leadership behavior. Your ethics will set the tone for the rest of your work group and your organization.

The Cause and Nature of Ethical Dilemmas

Ethical dilemmas often occur because a person's internal sense of right and wrong conflicts with a societal, cultural, professional, generational, or organizational ethical norm or belief. Each one of these ethical perspectives causes mental and emotional pressure on the individual to make choices or engage in certain behaviors which may or may be consistent with the individual's personal sense of right and wrong.

Ethical dilemmas also occur because a person will internally experience differing notions of what is ethical. At times, you might believe the right thing to do is to do what is best for you—promote your self-interest. On occasion, you may believe you ought to do what is best for others, pursue a more altruistic choice, and sacrifice your self- interest to help others. It is possible you will experience an inner knowing, an intuitive, unexplainable, feeling or conscience of what is right leading you to be true to your inner self. You may have a strong spiritual or divinely inspired notion of what is right and feel compelled to follow God's word as revealed in scripture or other holy writings. At times, you may feel societal or peer group pressure to do certain things. On many occasion, you might find yourself facing formal rules, codes of conduct, specified duties, or obligations requiring certain conduct from you. You might even feel all of these things at the same time, and try to balance these differing notions. You might select two or more of these inner conceptions and try to fulfill the ethical mandates within these choices.

Ethical dilemmas also occur when certain duties or obligations conflict with each other. For example, there are times when justice conflicts with mercy, a short term gain conflicts with a long range orientation, an individual's self interest's conflict with the interests of the larger community, or when truth conflicts with loyalty.

When you hear a person ask if a particular behavior is ethical, this is usually intended as an inquiry into which competing interest is to take priority. For example, in a given circumstance, is justice more important than mercy? Is concern for others to take precedence over self-interest? Is it more important that a person fulfill his duties or follow his or her intuitive sense or inner feeling? Should divinely inspired notions of right or wrong be used to resolve ethical issues arising in government or the military? These are the types of questions that ethics attempts to answer.

Developing a Personal Definition of Ethics

For some people, ethics isn't as abstract, esoteric, complex, or difficult as the scholars and academics make it out to be. For these folks, ethics is embodied in simple, practical and applied notions of right and wrong.

For them, ethics is understood as simple principles, formulations and beliefs, about how to live their lives, treat each other, seek profit, foster employee well being, and balance community and personal self-interests.

These folks know that their personal ethics are revealed in how they conduct their personal business, respond to trauma and disappointments in their lives, and act when no one is looking at them. They know that their ethics are revealed in the choices they make and in their behavioral responses to the defining moments that occur in their lives.

Do you have a practical, meaningful definition of ethics? Can you articulate what ethics requires of you in any given circumstance? Could you respond in a helpful, insightful way to your grandchild, son or daughter, niece or nephew, or close friend if they sought your advice on what ethics means?

My Definition

For me, ethics can be defined, simplistically, as those personal, freely chosen and consciously adopted beliefs, principles, or notions of what is right and wrong, how I ought to live my life, and more importantly, how I should treat other people.

Two important concepts are at the foundation of my

definition of ethics. The first is that ethics requires me to freely choose my beliefs and principles. This means that the beliefs and principles I choose must be uniquely mine, not those imposed upon me by others. The second is that my choice must be the result of a deliberate conscious decision and that I knowingly embrace the beliefs and principles that guide my life.

My personal concept of ethics also requires me to engage in personal conduct that exceeds or goes beyond the bare minimum requirements of the law and moves me closer to goodness and virtue. Thus, for me to be ethical, I must not simply conform my behavior to the minimum threshold requirements of the law; rather, I must engage in conduct that exceeds the law. I must act in a way that is virtuous and reflective of higher and nobler standards of right and wrong. My definition thus compels me to make decisions and engage in conduct that will move me closer to goodness and virtue in all that I do.

Implicit in this definition is that I must, at all times, comply with and obey all just laws. A just law is one that does not violate natural law or generally agreed-upon universal principles of right and wrong.

If a law is not just (for example, the laws that for many years in the United States encouraged and tolerated slavery, and subsequently, racial discrimination) my personal concept of ethics requires me to disregard or ignore that law. In doing so, however, I must be willing and prepared to accept the natural and logical consequences of my disregard for the law.

Admittedly, this is easier said than done. When push comes to shove, I honestly don't know how I would respond in such a situation. I do know, however, that my personal definition of ethics would better prepare me to respond in a virtuous manner. This definition would give me guidance and, hopefully, inspire me to act virtuously and with honor.

Your Personal Definition

I encourage you to reflect upon your personal definition of ethics. I encourage you develop, refine, and know the foundation of your ethics. I encourage you to connect with your notions of right and wrong. I encourage you to identify and articulate the criteria you use in discerning that which is right, and drawing the line between right and wrong. Your definition of ethics is an important beginning point in understanding the psychology of ethics, and it is one of the fundamental building blocks upon which the seven principles of ethical virtuosity are based.

Take the time now before reading further to discover and develop what ethics really means to you and what it requires of you as a person. Ask others for input. Discuss it openly with your loved ones. Challenge them to do the same. In doing so, you will acquire insight and a unique perspective for yourself.

*Laws are created
by humans as a means of
maintaining order in a society.*

CHAPTER 3

What Is Law?

I s there a difference between ethics and law? As you may recall, my personal definition of ethics makes a clear distinction between law and ethics. This demarcation is easy for me as a lawyer. For those untrained in the legal formalities and philosophical underpinnings of the law, the distinction is not so readily apparent or easily grasped. Consequently, a brief overview of the nature of law is presented as a means of helping you understand the differences between ethics and law.

Categories of Law

There are two major categories of law that must be pointed out in any in legitimate discussion of the nature and meaning of law. The first is "natural" law and the second is "man-made" law.

Natural law is embodied in those universal principles of right and wrong that transcend and endure the tests of time, cultural biases and historical forces. Natural law is God given and is discovered by study, contemplation, reasoning and reflection. Natural law includes principles such as:

- Murder is wrong
- Children should be protected
- Lying is wrong
- Incest is wrong

Natural law is similar to what I refer to as inherent, fundamental, ethical, or moral notions of right and wrong. As such, there isn't really much distinction between natural law, ethics and morality.

In contrast, man-made law is the written expression of a recognized authority vested with the power to make rules that govern, control and dictate the conduct of individuals and groups that comprise a society. As such, man-made law is created by humans as a means of maintaining order in a society. Man-made law is voluntary in nature and exists solely by agreement of the people. The people of a society voluntarily relinquish to a recognized sovereign or authority the power to create rules for the betterment of the society as a whole.

Protagoras, a Greek philosopher, observed that the law is a voluntary agreement between members of a society that restrains individual rights, liberty and behavior in order to maintain order and a civilized society.

In the United States, laws are made by four different types of authorities. The most commonly known law-making authority is the legislative body—a group of individuals elected by the people of a city, county, district, or state. The laws created by legislative bodies are generally referred to as "statutes."

Judges make law when they interpret statutes and declare or set forth rules they believe exist by virtue of the prior rulings of other judges. This type of law is known as "case" or "common" law.

The administrative and executive agencies of the federal government, as well as those of the fifty state governments, also make rules and regulations that have the force and effect of law. These administrative laws govern a variety of commercial activities such as safety, labor relations, food and drug processing, transportation, aviation, product safety, hazardous waste disposal, and truth and lending. The list of regulated activities is too voluminous to set forth in this modest treatment of the law. Suffice it to say that virtually every aspect of commercial activity has some federal or state agency that governs its conduct.

Law is sometimes made by the people through direct ballot initiatives, propositions, or referendums. These laws reflect pure democracy at work. Here, the law-making body is comprised of all people in a given jurisdiction who are entitled to vote.

Laws are enforced in several ways. The violation of some laws results in civil penalties, such as the payment of monetary damages to an injured or aggrieved party. The intent in such cases is to compensate the victim for the loss or harm caused by another's wrongful conduct. In other cases, the violation of a law can result in the imposition of criminal sanctions, such as a monetary fine, incarceration, or probation. In these cases, the intent is to punish the violator and deter others from engaging in similar illegal conduct.

Dual Nature of Law

By nature, law is both protective and restrictive. The Bill of Rights, for example, clearly is protective in nature, granting the individual citizen certain rights, such as freedom of speech, assembly, privacy, due process and religious freedom. On the other hand, zoning, land use, traffic, drug, abortion and gun control laws are viewed by many as deprivations and restrictions of individual liberty and freedom.

Naturally, a person's view as to whether law is protective or restrictive depends upon that person's particular circumstances, biases, prejudices and prior experiences with the law. A corporate executive may believe the law is too restrictive with respect to business matters and too liberal when it comes to the treatment of criminals. On the other hand, a poor and underprivileged person may believe that the laws regulating businesses do not sufficiently restrict corporate greed and power and those criminal laws overly restrict personal expression and freedom.

It is important to your understanding of the differences between ethics and law that you recognize the inherent dual nature of the of law and that you sort out the specific ways in which this duality is manifested in your behavior, thoughts, beliefs and feelings concerning the nature of law.

It is also important to recognize that ethics is not law and law is not ethics. In some cases, the law may mirror personal, organizational, cultural, societal, or professional ethics. In many cases and circumstances, however, the law will not coincide with personal, organizational, cultural, societal, or professional ethics.

Occasionally, people try to use the law to establish and impose a societal ethic. The twenty-first amendment to the United States Constitution which for a time prohibited the manufacture, distribution and sale of alcohol, is an historical example of using the law to impose a societal ethic. The prolific number of United States Supreme Court decisions on pornography, abortion, sexual preference and affirmative action are further examples of how far people will go to impose their personal notions of right and wrong on others through the manipulation and use of the law.

As a practical matter, and in most cases, however, law reflects minimum standards of civil behavior determined by an elected legislative body, judges and administrative agencies. A violation of the law is punishable by a fine or imprisonment. As noted above, ethical violations result in significantly different sanctions (e.g., personal anxiety, guilt, social ostracism, embarrassment, public scorn).

Beyond Law

As outlined in the previous chapter, I believe that ethics requires behavior that exceeds and goes above and beyond the bare minimum requirements of the law.

A good illustration of the distinction follows. Assume that you are the parent of a fourteen year old girl who aspires to become a member of one of the United States Olympic teams. Your daughter has natural talent and above average skills, but she needs additional work before she can achieve Olympic status.

She is invited to become a member of the United States National Junior Development Team, which is coached by a 36-year-old male who is highly regarded within the Olympic community. Your daughter accepts the invitation and trains for several months with the team. She, like the other members of the team, travels with the coach and is away from home for extended periods of time.

During one of her visits home she comments that the 36-year-old male coach is having sex with several of the older players on the team. Although the coach has not personally solicited or approached your daughter, she nevertheless expresses her concern and anxiety about the situation.

When you report the situation to the sport's governing body, an investigation is launched. The coach is open and candid about his affairs. He admits to having sex with several former and current players of the team, but asserts that the players were all over the age of 18 when the incidents occurred, and that each sexual relationship was consensual, voluntary and without harm to the girls.

The coach asserts that because the girls were over the age of 18, his actions were legal and in the absence of any specific organizational policy or rule forbidding sex between coach and player, his actions were permissible. He insists that he be exonerated from any legal wrong doing. Do you agree?

In most states, the law provides that the age at which a child becomes an adult is 18. As disturbing as it may seem, the coach's defense is legally correct. Although his conduct is legal, it is not necessarily ethical.

In 1896, the United States Supreme Court in a landmark case, *Plessy v. Ferguson*, held that the 14th Amendment to the United States Constitution (extending equal protection of the law to all U.S. Citizens) did not prohibit racial segregation practices. In other words discrimination along racial lines was allowable under a "separate but equal" standard of law.

The case arose in 1892, when a one eighth black shoemaker, Homer Plessy was jailed for sitting in a rail car designated for whites only. In upholding a Louisiana state law permitting these discriminatory practices, the Supreme Court validated the separate but equal legal doctrine which then became the legal standard for allowing other discriminatory practices such as prohibiting blacks from using "white only" separate toilet facilities, drinking fountains, rest rooms, schools, and sitting places on buses and in restaurants.

The separate but equal doctrine was the law of the land and permitted these notorious forms of discrimination for many years until overturned by *Brown v. Board of Education* in 1954. Although the segregational practices were found to be legal for many years, it cannot be said that such practices were ethical.

The same can be said of the practice of human slavery which for many years was legal throughout the United States and practiced by many founders of our country. Despite the fact that there are Biblical references endorsing slavery, can it be said that slavery is ethical, rational, or morally justifiable under any circumstance? The Books of Numbers and Deuteronomy contain many references concerning how one was supposed to treat one's slaves.

Think for a moment about the irony of the following clause found in the Declaration of Independence signed by our founding fathers, many of whom happened to own slaves at that time in history:

"We hold these truths to be self-evident, that all men are created equal, that they are endowed by their Creator with certain unalienable Rights, which among these are Life, Liberty and the pursuit of Happiness."

For some reason the founding fathers—men of great moral character—failed to see the fundamental unethical nature of human bondage. Although legal at that time in history, human slavery was most certainly morally objectionable and unethical.

The point being stressed here is that there is a difference between that which is legal and that which is ethical. Law sets forth certain bare, minimum, civil, and criminal standards of human conduct which may or may not coincide with that which is ethical.

Your Personal View of the Law

How do you perceive the law in the case of the volleyball coach? Does it adequately protect your daughter and other young girls from the sexual advances of the coach? Should it do so?

What are your attitudes regarding the law? Do you believe law is mostly protective of your civil rights, or is law restrictive of your personal freedoms? Do you believe law should mirror your personal ethics or should law reflect the personal ethics of others? Should law be used to impose ethical notions of right and wrong on others?

Your answers to these questions will provide valuable clues and insights into your ethical make-up. Spend a few moments in contemplation of what your responses reveal about you.

Ask others to do the same. Seek out their perceptions of the law and whether or not they believe there are differences between law and ethics. Listen and learn from their comments and observations. You might be surprised at how much you can gain from their individual and unique perspectives.

Chapter 4

What Is Integrity?

In the ethics classes and training sessions I have conducted over the years, I always have challenged the participants to define the concept of integrity. When I've done this, there generally has been a short and often uncomfortable pause as the participants look at me with puzzlement, shift in their seats and then divert their gazes away from me, fearing that if they make eye contact, I might call upon one of them to share their personal insights. I always stand patiently as they reflect upon and struggle with the difficult task of defining the salient characteristics and inherent nature of integrity.

What about you? Have you thought about integrity? Do you know what it really means? Do you know what it requires of you as a person? Do you have a definition of integrity that is meaningful, practical and relevant?

Take a moment, before reading further to jot down the initial thoughts and feelings that come to mind when you think of integrity.

Defining Integrity

Most of the students and seminar participants whom I've asked to define integrity have told me that integrity has something to do with "walking your talk," that it involves being "true to yourself," or that it means engaging in conduct that aligns with your inner beliefs, values and principles.

When I began conducting ethics training, I felt these formulations were pretty good. They were simple, easy to understand, helpful, meaningful, relevant and practical. Furthermore, the students and participants who came up with them genuinely liked their conceptions. They were proud of their ability to quickly and concisely capture the essence of integrity.

Upon deeper reflection, however, I realized that there are some notoriously unethical, immoral, and criminal characters that, under these definitions of integrity, would have to be classified as people of integrity.

For example, didn't Adolph Hitler "walk his talk" concerning his views and beliefs about the Jewish people? Didn't Timothy McVeigh, the Oklahoma City bomber, act in a way that was "true to himself"? Doesn't the criminal behavior of the inner city gang leader reflect and align with his inner beliefs, values and principles?

The notion that morally reprehensible people could have a virtuous trait attributed to them was unsettling to me. There was something disturbing about having to concede that unethical people like Hitler, McVeigh, and inner city gang leaders had integrity. I did not want to spoil the nobility of the concept by allowing the immoral and criminal to be considered people of integrity.

I did not like the definitions of integrity given to me by my students and seminar participants. I felt that something was missing. I felt that the definition of integrity needed to naturally exclude those deemed unethical by society from virtuous glow of integrity. I felt that the characterization of Hitler, McVeigh, the organized crime leader, and the inner city gang leader, as people of integrity, diminished integrity's inherent goodness.

In time, I turned to the dictionary for a rudimentary understanding of the word "integrity."

In doing so, learned that integrity is a noun that refers to a quality or state of unimpaired condition of being sound, whole, complete, undivided. Some dictionaries even include purity. I was reminded of the mathematical concept of the integer, which I remembered as being a natural or whole number. I discovered that some dictionaries include a secondary meaning for integrity, referring to it as the strict adherence to a moral code of values.

This information was interesting and somewhat helpful, but not satisfying in my quest for a better definition of integrity that took care of the Hitler, McVeigh and inner city gang leader problem.

My Definition of Integrity

I struggled for several years with this problem, trying to create a personally meaningful definition of integrity. I finally settled upon a concept that I now offer to you as a model, to consider in your discovery of what integrity means to you.

My definition of integrity now involves knowing my deeper, inner, authentic self and consciously choosing to act in a manner that is consistent with my personal ethical beliefs, principles and core ethical values. There are several individual elements of this definition.

First, my concept of integrity incorporates and builds upon my definition of ethics. Remember that my personal definition of ethics requires me to behave in a manner that exceeds the bare minimum requirements of the law and moves me closer to goodness and virtue. This component easily takes care of the Hitler, McVeigh, organized crime leader, and the inner city gang leader problem since their conduct does not conform to the law and does not reflect goodness and virtue. Thus, for me to be a person of integrity, I must do more than just "walk my talk." My beliefs and conduct must be inherently good and virtuous.

The second element is that if I am to be a person of integrity, I must have knowledge of my deeper, inner, authentic self. I must know who I am at my inner core. This knowledge must be unadulterated. I must, as Socrates implored, "know myself." This means knowledge and insight not only of my goodness and strengths, but also my weaknesses and darker components.

At another level, self-knowledge also requires that I have insight into my ethical constitution and belief system. I must know what ethics means and requires of me. I must know which ethical principles are important to me. I must know the core ethical values that guide my life.

The next element of my definition is that I must make a conscious, deliberate choice to behave in a manner that is consistent with my ethical beliefs, principles and core values.

In order for me to make such conscious choices, I must know, understand, appreciate and control my inner drives, ambitions, motivations, passions, emotions, desires, ego, temptations, weaknesses, vulnerabilities, rationalizations, denials, unconscious preferences and other hidden unknown influences—all of which, from time to time, obscure and prevent me from demonstrating, achieving and living integrity.

I refer to the above items as "barriers to integrity," since they get in the way of being a person of integrity.

Each of us has his unique and personal set of integrity barriers. Yours are different from mine. But don't kid yourself: you do have them. It's part of your inherent human nature. The challenge for you, and for all of us, is to know that these barriers exist, identify them, understand how they operate and master them by consciously choosing to disregard their negative influences.

Like most challenges in ethics, this is easier said than done. It is possible, and easier to accomplish once you have an understanding of the psychological forces that keep you from being a person of integrity.

Moment by Moment

I often ask students and seminar participants whether or not integrity is an absolute. In other words, is integrity an inherent trait that a person either possesses or lacks? Is integrity like being pregnant? You either are or you are not pregnant! Likewise, can't it be said that you are either a person of integrity, or you are not?

What do you think? Is integrity an absolute? Are you a person of integrity? To what extent do you genuinely live out your ethical beliefs, principles and values? Do these ethical notions move you closer to goodness and virtue? To what extent do others think you are a person of integrity?

I know that in my own life, there have been times

when I have compromised my ethical beliefs, principles and values and not been a person of integrity. I also know that there have been times when I have genuinely lived out and demonstrated integrity. I suspect that you can say the same for yourself.

I have concluded that integrity, for me, is an aspiration. It is something I must strive for on a moment by moment basis. Each dilemma I face, each crisis I encounter, every situation in which I find myself presents an opportunity to move closer to becoming a person of integrity. It is during these daily moments that I am tested and given the opportunity to achieve integrity. Isn't the same thing true in your life?

Dr. Andrew Pipe, Chairman of the Canadian Center for The Advancement of Ethics in Sports, made an insightful observation at a conference at which he and I once spoke. He said: "The difference between what you say and what you do, represents a loss of integrity."

In thinking about Dr. Pipe's observation, I offer the following modification. The difference between what you say are your ethical beliefs, principles and values, and what you actually do on a moment by moment basis represents a loss of integrity that can never be regained or replaced. You can only learn from these moment by moment losses and prepare for the next opportunity that is just around the corner. How you respond to these opportunities will determine the extent to which you achieve your integrity potential.

Classifications of Integrity

Just as there are six classifications of ethics there are six ways of looking at integrity—personal, cultural, societal, professional, generational, and organizational.

Being true to one's personal ethics would mean having personal integrity. However, being true to your personal notions of right and wrong, does not necessarily mean that you adhere to the ethical prescriptions of your culture and therefore have cultural integrity.

Remember, there are six classifications of ethics and when you act in strict accordance within the ethical parameters of one of these classifications, integrity exists and you may be said to have integrity within the confines of these classifications.

This is the reason for my disconnect with the gang leader being attributed with a quality of integrity. From my personal perspective, my ethics are different, but from the gang perspective of ethics, when the gang leader behaves in accordance with the gang's organizational ethics, he is being true to those organizational ethics, and by a strict and limited definition of ethics has integrity.

Your Definition of Integrity

If you want to prepare for the next opportunity for integrity, look back now on the initial thoughts you wrote down about integrity. Do those words feel adequate to you now in light of what you have read so far? Can't you make a few enhancements to your initial concept of integrity? What does integrity now mean and require of you? What are your unique barriers to integrity?

Character
is your moral personality.

CHAPTER 5

What Is Character?

Is there a person in your life perhaps a family member, friend, colleague, boss or subordinate, whose moral character you genuinely admire? Is there an historical, political, sports, community, spiritual or other public figure you think of as having great moral character?

If so, reflect for a moment and try to identify what it is about that person that causes you to think of him or her as a model of good character. What is it that sets that person apart from others? What one word best describes the essence of his or her character?

Do you know a person who lacks character? What is it about this person that is different from others? What distinguishes this individual from the person you regard as having character?

Your responses to this simple exercise should help you in defining and understanding the concept of character.

I have observed in my training sessions and in general discussions with leaders that many people use the word "character" in their conversations without much understanding of what it really means. Are you such a person? Can you honestly define and explain, in a meaningful and relevant way, to your son, daughter or other family member what character means?

Defining Character

I confess that I had a hard time coming up with my own definition of character. For many years, I was one of those people who used the word, but never really thought much about what it meant. When I began to reflect upon it, I realized how deficient my thinking had been.

As is my nature, I initially turned to the dictionary for help. I found that character has many meanings. I learned that character referred to a distinctive recurring pattern. I learned it originated from the field of lithography. I discovered that each individual letter of the alphabet was a distinctive character. I found that there were characters in a play or novel which portrayed certain recurring or distinctive roles that made them recognizable as the hero, protagonist, love interest, father figure, best friend, etc. I read that character also referred to a distinctive personal quality, mental and ethical traits, essential nature, notable traits, moral excellence, moral personality and moral strength. In a way, character is your collection of moral attributes—your moral essence.

Although I found these definitions helpful, I felt they

were limited in helping me to understand and discover something substantive and personally relevant about the concept of character.

After a period of patient contemplation, my thoughts and feelings on character slowly came forth from deep within my being. I share my concepts on character as a model for you to consider as you reflect upon what character means to you.

For me, character is a multi-dimensional concept that integrates my thoughts and feelings, conscious choices, free will and personal behavior.

Specifically, I define character in two ways.

First, I think of character as a person's moral personality, moral essence, or the inner dimensions of a person's being, spirit, or soul.

Character is the composite of all of your moral attributes as reflected in your choices and behaviors. Character is the distinctive end result of the interaction of your thoughts and feelings, your inner psychological drives and unconscious influences, tempered by your conscious choices (exercise of free will) and manifested, revealed and demonstrated by your personal conduct and behavior.

Another way of looking at character is to think of character as the distinctive impressions you make upon others and the resulting judgments people make about you. Have you ever had a great boss—a person who excelled at bringing out the best in you? Have you ever had a supervisor who was a terrible leader? When you thought about these two polar opposite personalities, didn't you make a personal judgment about each one of them? Your personal judgments were really your assessments of their character.

If you supervise others at work, you should know that your employees have made judgments about your character. As you live and encounter people in the world you make impressions upon them and they, in turn, make judgments about you and the nature of your character. They judge whether you are honest, trustworthy, genuine, reliable, caring, concerned about self, decent, honorable, etc. Your character is really within the hearts, souls, and minds of the people with whom we live, work, and play your families, friends, co-workers, employees, customers, etc.

In summary, Character is the collection of moral attributes within you, as well as, the judgments others make about you based upon choices and behaviors which have made impressions on them.

Life's Paradigm

My definition of character becomes clearer and more meaningful when you understand and appreciate what happens to you at a personal level as you live and experience the many challenging demands of life.

As you move through life, you encounter unique human challenges, demands, obstacles, dilemmas, disappointments, excitements, highs, lows, traumas, situations, hardships, joys and circumstances.

These life occurrences in turn trigger personal internalizations—inner processes and dynamics that happen deep within your heart, soul, mind and psyche. These internalizations take many forms, including but not limited to intense emotions, feelings, attitudes, thoughts, reflexes, reactions, defenses, denials, projections, unconscious judgments and preferences.

Internalizations happen automatically, quickly and in an unknowing, unconscious manner. We encounter a situation, and then, before we are even consciously aware of what has happened, we experience one of the many internalizations that are possible.

How many times have you, for example, said or done something as the result of an intense emotional reaction, perhaps anger or fear, which you later regretted? Isn't it true that if you had simply thought more about it, you would have acted much differently?

When internalizations occur, it becomes imperative that they be tempered with sound, rational, logical and conscious personal choices. If you fail to temper your internalizations, you will lose the opportunity to exercise your free will. You will remain a creature driven by emotional impulses, highly vulnerable to human weaknesses. By bringing to bear your capacity to reason, you will free yourself from your internalizations and create for yourself the opportunity to make personal conscious decisions that define who you are. Remember that all of your decisions are ultimately manifested, revealed and demonstrated in how you conduct yourself and behave on a day to day basis.

This is what I refer to as "Life's Paradigm." Daily life challenges trigger internalizations, providing you with the opportunity to define your character by your conscious choices and personal conduct.

Aristotle is known to have said that one's character is revealed not in one's speech, but in how one behaves. Buddha said that one's character is revealed not in times of comfort but during times of inconvenience and hardship. Looking at your behavior, then, is the key to discovering your character.

I have found it helpful to think of my character as being a "metaphorical piece of art" that is in a state of constant creation and perpetual evolution toward an ideal expression of who and what I am. As the single artistic creator of my character, I alone paint or shape and mold my character. In a sense, my character is projected outwardly from deep within me by the choices I make and by my behavior. The outward or external projection of my character is perceived by those with whom I live, work and play. Metaphorically speaking, it is within their hearts, minds and souls that my character is artistically created or given meaning or expression. Their hearts, minds and souls represent the canvas or artistic medium that gives my character life.

How Do You Define Character?

Please remember that my concept and definition of character is offered only as a model. I share it for the purpose of stimulating your personal contemplation of what character means to you. My definition works for me. It is relevant, helpful and meaningful as I encounter and face the ethical dilemmas that life presents to me.

I encourage you to begin the process of reflecting upon your concept of character. What does character mean to you?

The Character Continuum

Over the years, I have observed that people can be classified into common character types. The first way of classifying character is along a continuum ranging from weak moral character to strong moral character. I refer to this as the "Character Continuum." Think of a scale from one to ten. One represents weak moral character. Ten represents strong moral character.

Weak moral character exists when ethical traits are not consistently demonstrated in a person's behavior. A person of weak moral character has a set of ethical principles, but the principles are not generally well defined. A person of weak moral character often succumbs to internalizations and other vulnerabilities. He stumbles in times of ethical discomfort, moral ambiguity, or when moral courage is needed.

Strong moral character exists when ethical traits are consistently reflected in a person's behavior. A person of strong moral character has a well-defined ethical constitution and rarely succumbs to internalizations and other vulnerabilities. He is firm and unwavering in times of ethical discomfort, moral ambiguity, or when moral courage is needed.

Where would you place yourself on the continuum of moral character? About average (5)? Closer to strong moral character? Closer to weak moral character?

More importantly, where would others place you on this continuum? How would others describe your personal character? What will others remember and say about your character at your death?

Because of certain human tendencies, we are often unable to accurately perceive ourselves. It is difficult to see ourselves as others see us.

This phenomenon is known in psychology as the "fundamental attribution error" or the doctrine of "personal self deception." It is the attribution of desirable or positive traits to oneself which others do not necessarily believe you possess to the same degree.

The essence of your personal character is probably somewhere between where you perceive yourself on the character continuum and where others would place you.

The Hierarchy of Personal Morality

Another way of looking at character is on the "Hierarchy of Personal Morality." This is a concept I created as a way to help people understand where their personal ethical journey has taken them and where their personal moral path could lead.

The hierarchy consists of five classifications of moral character. The five categories are Morally Corrupt, Ethically Challenged, Legally Compliant, Ethically Striving and Authentically Virtuous.

A person who has a Morally Corrupt character, believe it or not, does have ethical beliefs, principles and values. The Morally Corrupt person possesses strong notions of what is right and wrong. Unfortunately, these notions are not embraced by the vast majority of society. The Morally Corrupt individual embraces beliefs, principles and values that generally result in socially reprehensible behavior such as criminality, violence and deviant personal conduct that is abhorrent to society.

A person who has an Ethically Challenged character totally lacks any sense or notion of right or wrong. It is as if the genetic material that is responsible for creating within a person a sense of right and wrong is missing and absent in the Ethically Challenged. This character type does not know what ethics is or what it requires. As such, the Ethically Challenged individual goes about his life completely oblivious to basic principles of morality.

Although the end behaviors of an Ethically Challenged person are similar to those of a Morally Corrupt person, there is a difference between these two character types. The Morally Corrupt person holds ethical beliefs that are intolerable to society. The Ethically Challenged individual does not even know it is possible to choose one's ethical beliefs, principles and values. Hence, the Ethically Challenged person has no personal code of ethics to which he can hold himself personally accountable.

The next character classification is Legally Compliant. This character is possessed by a person whose sense of right and wrong is derived from the bare minimum requirements of the law. The Legally Compliant individual makes no distinction between law and ethics. This person believes that a person has no duty, responsibility or obligation other than to obey and comply with the law.

The Legally Compliant person holds the belief that there is no higher, nobler standard of behavior. The Legally Compliant person equates ethics with the law. He believes that if it is legal, then it must be ethical.

Recall that this was the ethical view of the male coach referred to in Chapter 3, who slept with several of his female players after they turned 18 years of age. The coach rationalized his behavior by stating that since the girls were 18, they were adults and therefore, he had not done anything wrong. In other words, since he had broken no law, he believed his conduct was ethical. This is reflective of a person who possesses a Legally Compliant character.

A person who has an Ethically Striving character is one who is aware that there is a difference between ethics and law and who strives to demonstrate higher, more noble and virtuous principles in his daily conduct. The Ethically Striving person has a set of ethical principles, beliefs and values that are highly virtuous. Furthermore, he genuinely wants to abide by and demonstrate these principles in his life.

The Ethically Striving person has traveled farther than many who are on the journey toward ethical perfection. However, the path is steep, difficult and presents numerous challenges that often cause the Ethically Striving person to fall. Although this person may err from time to time, he will realize his mistakes, recover and continue to strive for ethical achievement.

The final and ultimate character classification is what I call the Authentically Virtuous. A person who is Authentically Virtuous has a strong sense of right and wrong. His ethical beliefs, principles and values are genuinely virtuous. He consistently lives them, demonstrating them in his decisions and conduct on a daily basis. The Authentically Virtuous rarely falters, and when he does, he holds himself accountable and accepts personal responsibility for his actions.

The most distinguishing aspect of the Authentically Virtuous is that others hold him in high regard. Others admire and hold him up as a model to be emulated.

The diagram on the opposite page depicts how the Hierarchy of Personal Morality looks.

In my view, the three character classifications to the left of the solid line (Morally Corrupt, Ethically Challenged and Legally Compliant) are unethical in nature, while those to the right of the line (Ethically Striving and Authentically Virtuous) are ethical and virtuous.

A Few Personal Questions

How do you assess your personal character? What is your moral essence? What is on the inside of you? Where do you think you fall along the Hierarchy of Personal

Morality? Morally Corrupt? I suspect not. Ethically Challenged? Possible, but not likely. Legally Compliant? A possibility. Many people have shared with me that they fall into this category. Ethically Striving? I hope so! Authentically Virtuous? Maybe.

Where do you think others would place you? Would where you place yourself be consistent with where others place you?

Of greater importance, what state of being do you desire to become? Is being Authentically Virtuous a desire? Is it a possibility?

The Character Continuum and the Hierarchy of Personal Morality are not, by any means, the only two ways of looking at character. There are numerous other perspectives. I offer these concepts simply as a means of motivating you to examine your personal character. What is most important for your own evolution is that you take an honest look at yourself and begin to make changes in your character.

The Hierarchy of Personal Morality

Unethical			Ethical	
Morally Corrupt	Ethically Challenged	Legally Compliant	Ethically Striving	Authentically Virtuous

*Some people
naïvely believe that ethics,
integrity and character
are not relevant
in our fast-paced,
modern society.*

CHAPTER 6

Why Are Ethics, Integrity, and Character Important?

Are ethics, integrity and character really important? Do these concepts make a difference in how you live your life, raise your family, conduct your personal business, or lead others at work? Is it possible that ethics is simply irrelevant, meaningless and insignificant? Do ethical concepts add anything to the quality of a person's life? Does an emphasis on integrity contribute anything to how we interact and work with each other? Does character count in the commercial jungle and intense economic warfare of the competitive corporate environment? Do ethical principles help you to increase revenue, control expenses, make a profit, or maximize shareholder equity and return?

Some people believe that the answer to these questions depends upon the life roles you are called upon to fulfill. There are those who believe that ethical considerations are a purely personal matter that should not be discussed or focused upon outside the home and personal relationships. Do you agree?

Aren't there common elements that exist across the various important roles you play in your life? Aren't ethics, integrity and character important in all of your activities?

What are your primary roles in life? Spouse? Parent? Employee? Supervisor? Entrepreneur? Professional? Director or trustee of an organization? Chief executive officer? Public servant? Elected official? Educator? Community leader? Government official?

If you are married, do you want and expect integrity from your spouse? If you are a parent, do you want your children to learn and demonstrate high ethical standards? If you are a supervisor, business owner, or chief executive officer, are you better off if your employees and subordinates are ethical and bring integrity and character to their jobs, rather than leave them at home? If you are a public servant, elected official, community leader, or director of an organization, is it true that those whom you serve expect you to perform your legal and fiduciary duties in an ethical manner?

Kouzes and Posner report in their seminal work, *The Leadership Challenge*, that most employees rank honesty as the most important leadership trait they want their bosses and leaders to possess.

This insight is the most significant reason that ethics, integrity and character are important. If you are to become a more effective leader, you must integrate ethical principles into your daily leadership behaviors.

Clearly, at a personal level, ethics, integrity and character are important and relevant. They give meaning and add quality and value to your relationships. The adverse, hostile environment in which you conduct business provides another important reason why ethics is vitally important. Consider the following.

Litigation is at an all time high. Juries now routinely return multimillion dollar verdicts. The financial, legal and personal consequences of employee misconduct, internal fraud, scandal, corruption and litigation are so devastating that failure to take aggressive, proactive and preventative measures can result in multimillion dollar judgments, bankruptcy, outrageous attorney fees, loss of public confidence, decline in employee morale, and loss of customer loyalty, tarnished reputations and destroyed careers.

It doesn't have to be that way. Ethics, integrity and character can prevent and deter unlawful and unethical conduct. Don't deceive yourself: the business and legal environment in which your organization operates is not friendly. It is a hostile and unforgiving climate.

Consider the following real-life examples as evidence of this madness.

Savings and Loan Fraud. In 1995, the Department of Justice reported that 5,506 former savings and loan officers, directors, CEOs, attorneys, accountants and consultants had been convicted of fraud in connection with the savings and loan fiasco. Of the 5,506 people convicted, 4,157 were sentenced to prison. Courts imposed fines of $45 million and ordered restitution of $2.9 billion.

Ford Motor Company. In 1995, a jury awarded $62.4 million to two women injured in a Bronco II rollover. $58 million was punitive in nature and based upon evidence that Ford allegedly hid evidence of the vehicle's deficiencies.

Phar-Mor. In 1995, Michael Monus, former president of Phar-Mor drug chain, was convicted of 109 counts of fraud.

United Way of America. In 1995, William Aramony, former president of United Way of America, was convicted in federal court of fraud and misappropriation. This was preceded by reports of Aramony's nepotism and excessive spending of donated dollars for first-class travel, private limousines and other luxury items.

Federal Government. In 1994 and 1995, the federal government spent $32.6 million on five independent counsel probes into ethics and law violations by a variety of government officials.

University of Miami. In 1995, the NCAA imposed

sanctions against the Miami Hurricanes that cost the university a football bowl appearance and a reduction of at least five scholarships each season through 1997. Additionally, Miami was placed on probation for three years and required to forfeit thirteen new football scholarships for the 96-97 season and eleven for the 97-98 season.

Bausch & Lomb. In October 1995, Daniel Gill, Chairman and CEO of Bausch & Lomb, was featured on the cover of Business Week. Inside, the cover story reported numerous instances of alleged questionable accounting practices and an alleged money laundering schemes. Two months later Mr. Gill resigned as Chairman and CEO.

Prudential Insurance Company. In 1996, it was reported that Prudential may be forced to pay up to $1 billion to resolve accusations of abusive sales practices by its insurance representatives. Recent press reports indicate that Prudential has offered $2 billion to settle claims against it.

Bankers Trust. In 1996, Bankers Trust Company agreed to pay $67 million to settle a dispute with Air Products over money-losing derivatives contracts.

Philadelphia Police Department. In 1996, ten lawyers and ten support staff were hired to work full-time to prepare a defense for the City of Philadelphia in a series of lawsuits associated with police fraud and scandal.

Westinghouse Electric. In 1995, a jury awarded four plaintiffs $64.65 million in an asbestos personal injury case.

TRW. In 1995, a jury awarded Talley industries $138 million in a breach of contract action originally brought by TRW against Talley Industries.

Columbia HCA. The United State's largest hospital chain became the target of a federal probe investigating alleged widespread fraudulent billing practices.

Texaco. Texaco was embarrassed by a racial discrimination suit when certain high-level officers were taped making racially disparaging comments and discussing the possible destruction of incriminating evidence. Texaco settled the claims by agreeing to pay $174 million.

State Farm Insurance. In 1996, a Utah jury returned a $147 million verdict against State Farm after hearing evidence of fraudulent and deceptive business practices.

Dow Corning. Dow Corning was forced into bankruptcy after three separate juries found it liable for injuries alleged to have been caused to three women as a result of Dow's manufacture and sale of silicone breast implants. The bankruptcy filing became necessary when an onslaught of additional claims were brought against Dow after the judgments were heavily publicized.

Enron. One of the world's leading firms, employing over 21,000 people, was forced into bankruptcy and liquidation when it was revealed that its financial performance was the result of accounting fraud and purposeful deception of shareholders by management.

Bill Clinton. While President of the United States, Bill Clinton, was impeached by the United States House of Representatives for his less than honest responses to questions posed by Special Prosecutor Ken Starr in connection with the Whitewater investigation probing Clinton's involvement with an Arkansas real estate development prior to being elected President. The more noteworthy and scandalous fact that emerged from this investigation was Clinton's sexual involvement with intern Monica Lewinsky, and his lying to the American public about the nature of his relationship with Lewinsky. Although the Senate did not convict Clinton of the impeachment charges, the damage to his marriage, credibility, reputation, and stature in history was profound.

Pete Rose. Legendary baseball player and team manager was banned from baseball as a result of his gambling in violation of baseball rules prohibiting such conduct.

Ted Haggard. Christian minister of a 14,000 member church and head of a nationwide Christian evangelical association resigned his positions after it was revealed he was involved in a homosexual relationship and used illicit drugs with a male "massage" therapist.

Kwame Kilpatrick. While imprisoned on charges of fraud, former the ex-mayor of Detroit was indicted on federal charges of bribery, corruption, extortion and fraud stemming from his activities as a member of the Michigan House of Representatives and as Mayor of Detroit.

Martha Stewart. The popular television personality and multiple business line promoter of food, fashion, and cooking products was charged, tried, convicted and served time in federal prison for illegal insider trading.

Michael Vick. The Atlanta Falcons and Philadelphia Eagles quarterback fell from public grace, served time in prison, and lost millions of dollars as a result of his personal role in financially sponsoring a dog fighting enterprise.

John Edwards. While running for President of the United States, it was revealed that candidate John Edwards was romantically involved with a woman who was not his wife at a time when his wife was suffering from incurable cancer. As a result of this peccadillo, Edwards's political chances for the office of President of the United States became zero.

Tiger Woods. The world's number ranked golfer and highest paid endorsement earner, Tiger Woods, suffered extensive financial losses, a broken marriage, and irreparable harm to his reputation as a result of his notorious sexual escapades during his marriage. Furthermore, the quality of Wood's golf game during the following year dramatically declined and he failed to win a major tournament—an unprecedented event in an otherwise spectacular career.

Kobe Bryant. Los Angeles baseball player was charged with sexual assault in a Colorado court stemming from his involvement with a young woman while recuperating from a medical procedure. His claims of being innocent sounded disingenuous to the world and hollow to his wife. Although he was able to repair the damage to his wife his image remains tarnished.

Ben Roethlisberger. This NFL quarterback for the Pittsburgh Steelers was suspended for the first four games of the 2010 season as a result of his behavior with several women who claimed he was sexually inappropriate during his frequent visits to night clubs in the prior year.

The cases cited above are not isolated examples. Although they are noteworthy, they represent only the tip of the iceberg. Every day, in courtrooms all across America, similar verdicts are rendered against organizations and individuals resulting from the absence of ethical principles, organizational integrity and character. A more significant fact is that an unknown number of lawsuits are settled everyday in order to avoid the adverse publicity that would result from public disclosure of wrongful conduct. Almost daily we read in the paper about some celebrity, politician, or athlete who has behaved in an unethical manner. And for those of us who work in business, we observe questionable conduct by others more frequently than ever before.

Some people naively think that employee misconduct, fraud, scandal, corruption and litigation are not genuine threats to their organizations. These people mistakenly believe that they are somehow immune and that they and their organizations are not at risk. This belief is not reasonable. A simple review of major litigation in America indicates that many reputable organizations and executives have suffered the embarrassing and debilitating effects of fraud, scandal, corruption and litigation—the results of an absence of ethics, integrity and character.

Don't be a victim of your own self-deception. The threat is real. As the leader of your organization, department, or work unit, you are at risk if ethics, integrity and character are not top priorities. Just remember, any one of your employees could easily cause you to become an unwitting victim of misconduct.

Ethics, integrity and character are also relevant if you want to:

- **Demonstrate and Reflect** your personal commitment to and expectation of ethical behavior.

- **Promote and Encourage** sound ethical decisions and responsible behavior.

- **Prevent Litigation** and the waste of time, effort, energy and money on ill-advised lawsuits.

- **Preserve the Public's Confidence** in your organization, your products and your services.

- **Provide an Organizational Conscience** that helps employees to responsibly face and overcome the ethical challenges they will encounter in your service.

- **Improve Employee Morale** by strengthening your organization's relationship with your employees.

- **Provide a Framework** for understanding that ethical dilemmas can and should be confronted and resolved in a thoughtful and meaningful manner.

- **Save Your Money** for years to come.

- **Protect Your Profitability** and preserve your bottom line.

- **Reduce the Threat** of employee misconduct, fraud, scandal, corruption and litigation.

If you believe ethics, integrity and character are not relevant to you and your organization, you are vulnerable to the following consequences:

- Losing your career
- Tarnishing your reputation
- Paying multimillion dollar judgments

- Paying outrageous attorney fees
- Losing the public's confidence in you and your organization
- Losing customer loyalty
- Experiencing adverse publicity, embarrassment and humiliation
- Suffering declining profits, diminished shareholder returns and loss of equity

A Few Personal Questions

What do you think about ethics, integrity and character? Are they important, relevant and meaningful concepts for you? Do you even care about such things? What will you do as you go forward in your career about ethics, integrity and character.

CHAPTER 7

Can Ethics Be Taught?

One of the controversies that exists in the academic and professional world is the question of whether or not ethics can be taught. There is little dispute that ethics can and should be taught to children by their parents. There is disagreement, however, with respect to whether ethics can or should be taught in settings outside the home.

In almost every ethics class or training session I have taught, there has always been at least one student who insisted that the ethics class was meaningless and a total waste of tuition and time. I've also had discussions with a small number of business executives who maintain that ethics training makes little or no difference in the bottom line performance of an adult employee.

The rationale for these views is that the adult employee or student has an unchangeable ethical belief system or character that cannot be influenced by any ethical knowledge acquired during adulthood.

Those who hold this view believe that a person's character is set in stone during childhood, and that an ethics class or a mandatory ethics training module is simply "too little, too late." The view does not dispute that ethical knowledge can be taught or transferred. It simply says that teaching ethics does not make a difference in the lives or conduct of people.

This view represents a rather narrow and pessimistic view of human potential. It disregards the fact that human beings have free will, the uniquely human ability to choose how to respond to difficult situations and circumstances.

Because you have free will, you possess the ability to make conscious choices as to how you will behave. If this were not so, your human behavior would be nothing but a series of hopelessly unchangeable, conditioned reflexes emanating from your childhood experiences.

This is not to say that your developmental history is an insignificant factor in how you behave in a given situation. Your childhood experiences with family, friends, school and church do indeed influence your behavior and emotions. They do not, however, cause a total shut-down of your human autonomy or free will.

The experiences of Victor Frankl and other holocaust survivors illustrates the enduring quality of human free will and the resilient ability of humans to choose dignity and life in a situation of human depravity. It is this same human quality that allows you to choose enlightened and responsible behaviors as an adult.

Furthermore, your intellectual, emotional, moral and spiritual components are constantly evolving. They change in response to new knowledge and worldly experience. You need only look at your own life and experiences to see the growth and change that occurs. Consequently, teaching ethical knowledge, principles, concepts, belief systems, decision-making models and analytical techniques can influence this natural process of individual human evolution and growth.

Granted, teaching ethical knowledge may not necessarily cause you to act more ethically. The knowledge will, however, help you to recognize, understand and appreciate that all ethical dilemmas present options and choices, some of which are more noble and desirable than others. Ethical knowledge will give you a better framework from which to analyze an ethical dilemma and consciously choose a path that will lead you to a virtuous solution.

Often, the reason some people believe ethics, integrity and character cannot be taught is that they unconsciously fear that the ethics curriculum will challenge their fundamental beliefs of right and wrong or impose upon them a specific ethical view or perspective. I must caution you that there are many ethicists who try to do this very thing. They self-righteously believe they have found the essence of ethical truth and knowledge, and they try to impose their perspectives on others. This is not what ethics ought to be about. Ethics, in my view, is helping people to make informed, conscious decisions to move closer to goodness and virtue.

The teaching of ethics is much like the teaching of music. The essential foundations, theories, principles and techniques can be taught. It is up to you, however, to use that knowledge of music theory to create music rather than noise. Likewise, the teaching of ethical knowledge can result in either virtuous or unethical behavior. Clearly, the choice to act ethically is entirely up to you.

Another interesting question that arises from time to time in my ethics classes is whether or not the ethics of people change over time?

While a student at the University of Chicago, Lawrence Kohlberg began studying and developing the concepts of Swiss psychologist Jean Piaget regarding personal moral development.

Kohlberg's theories suggest that people move through various stages of development and that a person's ethics can and do change over time for many people. Kohlberg theorizes that there are three major developmental levels of moral development.

The first level of moral development was labeled by

Kohlberg as the Pre-Conventional Level of moral reasoning where the ethics of an action is determined by its direct consequences of the action and how those consequences affect oneself. In this stage, there is no concern for societal norms or concerns for others. Ethics are grounded upon self-interest—doing what is best for the decision maker.

Kohlberg called the second level of moral development, the Conventional Level of moral reasoning. At this level, a person determines right from wrong by taking into account societal customs, norms, views and expectations. At this level of moral development, greater emphasis is placed on following rules, fulfilling expectations, obeying rules, and fulfilling duties associated with various . According to Kohlberg this is done in order to be liked, accepted, and deemed relevant in society.

Kohlberg's third level of moral reasoning is known as the Post-Conventional level where people begin to understand the gift of individual autonomy, the right to choose and live their lives based upon higher principles. In this stage, people begin to take into account the needs of others. They may disobey rules which conflict with their self interested notions of right and wrong. At this level principles, values, and rights are the foundations for knowing right from wrong.

Kohlberg also theorized that there may be a fourth

level of moral development which he referred to as Transcendental Morality, or The Morality of Cosmic Orientation—a level of moral reasoning based upon religion, spirituality, and divine inspiration.

My observations and personal experiences suggest that Kohlberg's theory of moral development is valid. I see young children, who naturally are preoccupied with self, grow into young adults who begin to develop awareness of others and try to accommodate the interests of those with whom they live. I see young teens grow, mature, and begin to follow social norms, fulfill roles in society, and obey the rules of life. Over time, I see how these young people begin to self-individuate, listen to the inner stirrings within themselves, and develop personal values and principles. I also see how many people hear the call of spirituality or experience the divine inspiration of God as they search for what is and is not right in our lives.

In essence, the levels of moral reasoning described by Kohlberg have real life correlates in the world. These levels of moral reasoning support the notion that ethics can be taught, and that ethics change and evolve within each one of us.

The question for you is how do you weigh in on this subject? Do you believe ethics can be taught? Do you believe your ethics change over time? Do you think that your ethics or those of other people evolve along a continuum of ethical development? What stage of Kohlberg's theory of moral development best describes your ethical core? Pre- Conventional stage centered upon self interest or self preservation? Conventional stage focused on others? Post Conventional stage in which decisions are grounded on higher principles and values? Transcendental Morality with religion or spirituality as the basis for ethical decisions?

The decision you make
when confronted with
an ethical dilemma is
a function of many factors.

CHAPTER 8

Where Do Ethical Beliefs Originate?

Do you have an opinion about any of the following controversial topics?

- Abortion
- Capital punishment
- Gun control
- School prayer
- Physician assisted suicide
- Gay rights
- Stem cell research

I suspect that you have a strong opinion about each one of these issues. Choose the one issue about which you feel most strongly. Put the topic firmly and squarely in your mind.

What is your opinion on the issue you have chosen? Do you favor it? Do you oppose it? What are your feelings concerning how this issue ought to be resolved?

More importantly, can you identify the origin of your beliefs and judgment concerning the issue you have selected? In other words, where does your belief on the chosen topic come from? What factors have influenced and determined your judgment?

There are several factors that affect how you feel about a controversial issue or ethical dilemma. These factors probably include parental upbringing, religious or spiritual teachings, peer pressure, education, role models, cultural influences, societal pressures, law, the media and your worldly experiences. Are you aware of the extent to which each of these factors has contributed to your ethical judgments of what is right and wrong?

Most people report that their parents have had an important influence in how they resolve ethical dilemmas. Sometimes a person discovers that he has become very much like his parents when it comes to ethical values, principles and beliefs. Although it may not seem likely during adolescence and during early adulthood, it is not uncommon for a person to ultimately adopt and hold ethical views and opinions that are remarkably similar to those of his parents.

In many cases, there is no similarity. There is overt disagreement. In these cases, the parental influence has been to drive the child to adopt and hold beliefs vastly different from the parent in an attempt to achieve individuation and differentiation. Nonetheless, the parent has contributed to the child's adult judgments.

Religious and spiritual teachings may also influence how you resolve ethical dilemmas. Because of the inherent judgments of morality contained in religious doctrine, your religious experiences tend to have a profound influence on your ethical responses and choices when you are confronted with an ethical dilemma.

Likewise, your educational background and experiences affect how you resolve ethical dilemmas. More often than not, a military academy graduate thinks and feels differently than a liberal arts college graduate. A business major approaches ethical dilemmas differently than does an art or music major. A person with no college education will most likely have an even more diverse approach and value system. Each of these academic disciplines values different principles, thoughts and feelings concerning what are important in life and how one ought to treat other people. In essence, education provides the opportunity for unique and diverse insights that may not otherwise be readily available.

Peer pressure is another influence that must be recognized. There is a natural human tendency to want to be accepted and admired by one's peers. This proclivity is particularly strong during adolescence. In many cases, a person carries this tendency well into adulthood. It is expressed in many subtle ways, such as wanting to have the right car, belonging to the right social or country club, buying the latest clothing fashions, sending your children to acceptable schools, or socializing with the right people. It is not surprising that in many ethical dilemmas, people will conform their choices and behavior to those their peer group would find acceptable.

The media's portrayal of certain types of conduct, such as violence, coarse language, sex, love, marriage and divorce, also contributes to how you think about and view the ethical dilemmas you encounter. Television and movie productions have had a subtle but profound influence on how an entire generation thinks and feels about certain life situations and personal behavior.

Your personal experiences also shape and determine how you resolve ethical dilemmas. A person who has been the victim of a heinous crime most likely has views about the death penalty and gun control that are different from those of a liberal college professor. A person who has watched a parent or other loved one suffer the ravaging and painful effects of a terminal disease that takes away the victim's humanity and dignity most likely has intense feelings about physician-assisted suicide—particularly when a parent or loved one has stated his preference for a dignified end.

The influences that affect your ethical preferences and

choices are numerous. They occur consciously and unconsciously. The unconscious influences are also known as our internalizations, discussed in Chapter 5.

There are two other sources of ethical beliefs that I've not yet discussed, but which are of great importance. They are conditioned reflexes and reflective judgment.

Conditioned reflexes are the end result of your personal internalizations described in Chapter 5. They are your unthinking behavioral responses to the ethical challenges, demands and circumstances you encounter. They are automatically triggered by certain hot spots and vulnerabilities that result from your prior experiences. Everyone experiences conditioned reflexes. They happen frequently and occur unconsciously. But with practice, insight, understanding and emotional discipline you can minimize and even control your conditioned reflexes.

The biggest challenge is to become aware of your conditioned reflexes as they occur. Can you identify when you experienced an unthinking, conditioned reflex? What was the trigger? What was the emotional hot spot that set you off? Do any of your ethical judgments pertaining to abortion, capital punishment, gun control, school prayer, physician assisted-suicide, or gay rights result from a conditioned reflex?

Reflective judgment is another source of ethical beliefs. Reflective judgment is a disciplined, deliberate process of pausing, reasoning, weighing the alternatives and sorting out various internalizations and conditioned reflexes in order to engage in rational thinking and judgment before acting. Most of us don't do enough reflective judgment, if any at all.

If you are to achieve ethical virtuosity, you must become aware of your individual influences, understand how they affect your choices and put them into perspective by engaging in reflective judgment.

To be able to do this, you must answer a few questions about yourself. What are the dominant ethical influences in your life? Family? Peers? Education? Media? Worldly experience? Religious teachings? Conditioned reflexes? Reflective judgment?

CHAPTER 9

Why Do Good People Act Unethically?

Have you ever wondered why people engage in unethical conduct? Are you aware of why you have acted unethically in the past? Here are a couple of true stories that might help you to find the answers to these questions.

The Bowling Proprietor

Members of a small church approached a bowling alley and made arrangements for the church to conduct a bowling league for its members. The bowling alley and the church verbally agreed to the arrangements. No written agreement was signed.

A few days prior to the commencement of the church's bowling league, the proprietor notified the church that the church's bowling league could not be conducted on the agreed upon day and time. The reasons given were that the proprietor could rent the bowling lanes promised to the church to a much larger group, for a longer period of time, and that the larger group would be heavy consumers of food and drink, whereas the church group would not. The proprietor admitted he had promised the lanes to the church for its bowling league, but nonetheless, he breached his promise to the church and refused to honor his commitment.

Do you believe the bowling proprietor acted unethically in refusing to honor his promise to the church? I suspect that you will agree with me that the proprietor acted in an unethical, unfair and dishonest manner. Most people hold to the principle that promises and commitments to customers and clients should be kept, and that a subsequent opportunity for additional profit does not justify the failure to keep a prior commitment or promise.

After hearing of this occurrence and concluding that the proprietor was unethical in his behavior, I became intrigued by several other questions.

Specifically, I wondered what motivated the proprietor to act in such a manner. What was his thought process as he canceled the church's bowling league? What went on inside his mind, heart and soul as he breached his promise to the church? Was the motivation greed? Financial necessity? Ignorance? Did the proprietor believe that the consequences of breaching his promise would be nominal? Did he think that his behavior was justified by the increased profit derived from the larger group?

You and I will never know the specific thoughts of this proprietor. I considered, briefly, the possibility of calling him and asking him to share with me the rationale for his decision. Fortunately, common sense overcame my impetuous curiosity, and I wisely chose to reflect instead on the safer, deeper and more general question of why good people engage in unethical conduct.

The Seller of an Industrial Building

A real estate investment firm seeking to make acquisitions of commercial real estate found an industrial building for sale in Loveland, Colorado. The seller verbally agreed to sell the building to the real estate investment firm at an agreed price of $10,250,000. A letter of intent was signed by the buyer and seller which provided that a legal contract would be drawn up, and if the legal aspects were agreed to by both parties there would be a sale at the agreed price.

The parties met each other, shook hands and proceeded to have the legal contract drafted. The written contract was reviewed and verbally agreed to by both parties. The day before the contract was to be signed; the seller refused to proceed with the signing saying that he now believed his property was worth an additional $800,000 which he demanded the buyer pay. His rationale for not keeping his promise was that he believed the property was worth more than the price he agreed to sell to the buyer.

Do you think this rationalization is ethical? Do you think the seller acted ethically?

Under most state laws a verbal agreement for the sale of real estate cannot be enforced unless all the material terms had been reduced to writing and signed by the parties. Here the only writing was the letter of intent signed by the parties which provided the transaction was not binding until a contract embodying the legal terms had been negotiated and signed.

Under this set of facts, did the seller act in an *unethical* manner? Hadn't he made a promise and then broken that promise? The legal contract had been drafted and agreed to, but at the last minute the seller changed his mind with respect to the previously agreed upon price and now demanded more money. Was this right or wrong conduct by the seller?

The Promotion Story

A fifty-five year old middle management executive of a nationwide company with close to 25 years of excellent employment with his company had a dream. He desired to be promoted to a vice president and finish his career with his company with greater professional prestige and a substantially higher retirement income. On a scale of one to ten, with ten being high, he rated his desire to be a vice president as a ten.

This executive had lived in the same town for his entire career. He loved his home town and never thought of leaving the area. Using the same ten point scale, he rated his desire to remain in his hometown at a ten.

During the last five years, the executive applied for every vice president position in his company that became available in his hometown. There were four such positions.

Each time, the executive was selected as one of three finalists, but on each occasion the promotion went to someone else. His disappointment was great but never reached a level of anger or intolerance. He understood at some level, that those chosen for the vice president positions were, in fact, better qualified and more suited for the promotion than he. Nonetheless the executive was becoming more anxious, frustrated, and impatient.

The executive was chosen to participate in a senior management leadership development course. The program included several sessions with an executive career coach. During these coaching sessions, the executive related his desire for a promotion, his experiences in being selected a finalist, but never getting a position. The coach suggested that perhaps the executive should broaden his career horizons and apply for other vice president positions at other geographical divisions and offices of the company located outside of his hometown. The executive related his conflicting desire to remain in his home town. The coach understood, but gently reminded the executive that sometimes in life sacrifices had to be made in order to acquire other things which were desired.

A few weeks later, another vice president position opened up in his home town office. When his boss made him aware of the position, he also mentioned to him another position that had just opened in the Bemidji, Minnesota, office. Knowing of the executive's desire for a promotion and aware that time was running out for the promotion of the executive, the boss suggested that the executive should consider applying for both positions.

The executive took his boss' advice and applied in both places despite the fact that Bemidji had long, cold, and harsh winters that were not appealing to him. The executive landed interviews in his home town and in Bemidji.

The executive's visit to Bemidji, at the company's expense, was pleasant despite the extreme coldness, gray skies, and rural setting of the company offices. He met the mayor of Bemidji and was given a grand tour of the area by helicopter, arranged by and paid for by the

Bemidji area executive in charge. Other than the climatic and geographical conditions, he thought Bemidji was an okay, but not desirable place to live and work.

The executive's interview in his home town was pretty much the same as his prior interviews. Several weeks passed before he received notice from his boss that he did not get the promotion in his home town. Later that same day he got a call from the Bemidji executive in charge asking him to come up for another interview. He reluctantly agreed to go. He did so with the feeling that he really had no other option. Additionally, the words of his executive coach echoed in his mind, reminding him of what it takes to achieve goals.

At the end of the Bemidji visit, he was offered the position, and in a moment of emotional weakness, he accepted the job and agreed to report to Bemidji in three weeks.

When the executive arrived home late that night, he was greeted by his loving spouse who asked how he enjoyed Bemidji. He told his wife that it went well, he had been offered the promotion in Bemidji, and he had accepted the job on the spot because he felt he had no other options if he was to achieve his goal of being a vice president.

The wife was shocked and become angry with him because she felt she had not been given an opportunity to participate in the decision. Things did not go well in that conversation.

The wife screamed at him: "What were you thinking! How could you make such a decision without consulting me? You know I do not want to leave this town!"

The executive replied curtly: "What were you thinking? You knew I went to Bemidji the first time, knew I was going the second time, and never said anything at all to discourage me or tell me you would not support me going to Bemidji. How could you do that to me and not communicate your desires?"

The wife blurted out in frustration: "You have been passed over four times for a promotion here in your own office. I thought who in their right mind, regardless of where the job was located, was ever going to give you a promotion. I just figured it would be a non-issue!"

The rest of the night was not pleasant around the executive's home. When he went to work to next day, he was called into the boss' office. His boss told him he had some bad news and some good news. The bad news was that the person selected for the home town position had died yesterday while the executive was in Bemidji. The good news was that the boss was going to promote the executive to be the new vice president. The boss made a passing remark to the executive: "It's a good thing those folks in Bemidji are so slow and never got around to offer-

ing you a job in Bemidji since that would really compli-
cate things a bit."

What do you think the executive decided to do? Keep
his promise to go to Bemidji? Accept the job in his home
town and break his promise to the Bemidji executive in
charge?

What do you think is the right thing to do? What
would you do?

This story is one that I often tell in my ethics sessions.
I will personalize the story and ask the participants to
decide what they would do if they found themselves in
such a scenario. Over 90 percent of the participants in
my classes, without hesitation, decide to accept the job in
their home town and break their promise to go to
Bemidji. Only a few honor their word.

Most of those who indicate they would accept the job
in their home town, relate to me a feeling of uncomfort-
ableness and much guilt in doing so. They confess that
they know they are breaking a promise, but justify their
decision in many creative ways, such as saying: "Things
have changed; Bemidji will understand." Or: "I won't be
happy in Bemidji; An unhappy person is not productive
so it is better for all if I do not go to Bemidji, regardless of
my promise." Or: "I have to take care of my family."

What really causes most people to go back on their
word? What are you thinking at this moment? Can you

figure out what your thoughts and reactions to this scenario reveal about the nature and quality of your ethical beliefs?

What possessed Tiger Woods to act the way he did during his marriage? What motivated the Enron executives to engage in financial accounting fraud? What factors caused young men and woman of the United States army to behave at the Abu Grav terrorist detention center in a manner that most Americans found shocking? What motivated the judge in Paris Hilton's jail incarceration review to release her from jail early? Was it undue influence, duty, economic pragmatism, justice, favoritism, or mercy?

Personal Reflection

Most people think of themselves as being a good person. When I ask my ethics session participants to raise a hand if they are a good person, everyone with a bit of encouragement will raise their hands. I raise my hand and remark to them that I think of myself as a good person trying to do good in my life.

I immediately follow this question by telling my class participants to raise a hand if you have never acted unethically. The response to this instruction is silence with no one raising a hand. People shake their heads, glance downward, and avoid making eye contact with me. There is some uneasiness which is often broken by an occasional smile or soft laughter.

I then tell the class members to raise a hand if you will never act unethically in the future? I get the same silence, no hands, and a few smiles with a comment that we are all human!

I am intrigued by this response because it illustrates that good people act unethically, and that good people will act unethically in the future. I am curious as to what motivates good people to violate their own ethical codes of conduct, particularly since most people have already told me early on in my ethics session that they have ethics.

Think for a moment about a time when you violated your own sense of right and wrong. Recall an incident in your life when you consciously acted unethically. Ask yourself what circumstances did you face at that time? What motivated you to act the way you did?

Over the years, folks have openly shared with me the motivations for their unethical conduct. Here is what I have learned.

Ignorance

Some people are genuinely ignorant of what is right and wrong. Incredibly, these people do not know what is ethically expected of them in certain situations. This results from a variety of factors, including but not limited to absence of a sense of right and wrong, lack of a personal conscience, character deficiency, no positive role model, absence of an applicable code of ethics, failure to know of the existence of an appropriate code of conduct, failure of the code to address the specific issue, and failure of an organization or trade association to develop and/or clearly communicate a standard of ethical behavior.

No One Will Find Out

There are some people who are aware that a particular course of conduct is unethical, but they consciously choose to engage in wrongful behavior due to a belief or perception that no one will ever discover or learn of it. The notion here is that if you can get away with it, you might as well do it.

Ends Justify the Means

There are many intelligent people who, when faced with a difficult choice or decision, will consider the end result they hope to achieve in relation to the harm that will occur if they act unethically in order to achieve it. In this deliberation, they will choose the course of action that will accomplish their desires, regardless of the harmful consequences that will occur if their unethical means are detected, made known, or exposed. People who use this rationalization often explain that their unethical conduct "was a necessary evil" in order to achieve their end result.

Inexplicably, unethical conduct has sometimes resulted from the notion that an ethical standard can and should be breached in order to advance or promote a higher or nobler cause or principle. This was the rationalization of those involved in the Watergate and Iran-Contra controversies. Both the Watergate conspirators and Iran Contra operatives engaged in unlawful, unethical conduct in a vain, desperate and misguided effort to advance what they believed were critical national interests and policies.

Nominal Consequences

Some people are aware that a particular behavior is unethical, but consciously choose to engage in the wrongful conduct due to a perception that the consequences will be minimal. The feeling here is that being caught will not be harmful. The nominal consequences belief is a variation of the "ends justify the means" rationalization. It differs from the ends justify the means concept in that the consequences expected are perceived as being nominal and not likely to occur.

Others Do It

Sometimes, unethical conduct is justified by the notion that others are doing it, so it really can't be that bad—or if I don't do it, I'll lose a competitive advantage in the marketplace.

This belief is a primary reason we are witnessing and experiencing predatory and deceptive trade practices. It is also the reason why many of our athletes have turned to performance-enhancing drugs. They perceive that their competitors are using these substances and that they cannot compete unless they create a level playing field by also getting the advantages such drugs afford.

Relative Filth

Some unethical conduct occurs because people believe that there behavior is "not so bad" when compared to the conduct of others who have engaged more egregious behavior. During the Abu Grav incident where US soldiers serving as guards at the terrorist detention facility placed naked prisoners in human pyramids, photographed them without clothes, sexually taunted them, and exposed the prisoners to vicious dogs. An army general commented to the media that this conduct was not particularly out of line when compared to the video release of terrorists beheading and mutilating US soldiers who had been captured.

Although the nature of the Abu Grav conduct clearly was not as "filthy" as that of the terrorist beheading of US soldiers, the conduct cannot be justified or diminished by comparison. The notion of relativeness should not be allowed to motivate or justify unethical conduct since the behavior inherently is unethical, regardless of its relative goodness in comparison to other unethical acts.

Prior or Current Perceived Unjust Harm

There are occasions when people believe they are victims of a prior or current unjust harm, and that this unfair treatment justifies their own unethical conduct. This is akin to the notion of balancing or making even the playing field. I've had students, business executives and seminar participants readily admit that because they felt underpaid or otherwise mistreated by a boss or supervisor, they intentionally padded an expense account as a means of obtaining just compensation.

The most drastic and extreme form of this belief is the increasing frequency of workplace violence that is now occurring, not to mention the senseless rage killings which have occurred in or schools and colleges by people claiming to be victims of bullying, or other forms of mistreatment.

Unrealistic Demands and Pressure

Unethical conduct is often caused when an employer places unrealistic demands or pressures upon employees who are unable to meet the deadlines or performance standards. Such pressures encourage and tempt employees to bend the rules in order to avoid the harsh consequences of failing to meet a deadline or standard. In these circumstances, the perception is that the consequence of not meeting the deadline or business goal is far greater than the harm suffered from the unethical conduct. Hence, it seems better to act in an unethical manner than rock the boat and be exposed to the possibility of losing one's job.

Financial Necessity

Unethical conduct is sometimes motivated by the threat of economic or financial disaster. People occasionally find themselves financially strapped and in need of money that they cannot obtain in a lawful or legitimate manner. Consequently, they seek other means of meeting their basic economic needs.

Low-paid law enforcement officers, who work incredibly long hours in a high-risk job are particularly vulnerable to such pressures. The belief is that a little unethical conduct is nothing compared to the personal need for money in order to survive. Many small-time embezzlers have admitted that a personal financial crisis, coupled with opportunity, was the major reason why they stole from their organizations.

Egoism

Egoism refers to self-centered decision making and conduct without regard for other people. Often, unethical conduct results from a person's failure to accommodate or consider the needs of other people. When this is coupled with avoiding personal accountability for one's actions, unethical and wrongful conduct is inevitable.

Egoism is also sometimes referred to as self-interest or self-preservation. The thought is that there is a natural human trait or tendency to take care of ourselves before taking care of others.

Many believe this preoccupation with self is hard wired into us and is a natural response when we feel threatened. When traveling in a commercial airline we are instructed in case of an oxygen failure to place the oxygen mask over our face before trying to assist children elderly or others in need. Our immune system is a naturally occurring self-preservation defense mechanism that activates to kill intruders (harmful bacteria and viruses) in our bodies. Life guards are taught to always protect themselves by physical force or by submerging when rescuing a drowning person in need of assistance. The reason is that the self-protective instincts of the drowning person is to grab and climb on to the rescuer and push the rescuer under water as a platform to remain above water.

Without a doubt, egoism and self-interest are large determinants of unethical conduct. Unfortunately, self deception keeps us from recognizing our own egoism. We see it in others, but have a hard time acknowledging it within ourselves.

It's Not Illegal

There is a notion that if a certain conduct is not prohibited or banned by law, then it is permissible to engage in that conduct. This was the rationale of the sports development coach, discussed in Chapter 3, who felt it entirely acceptable for him to have sex with his female players as long as they were 18 years of age. It is also the rationale of the legalized houses of prostitution in Nevada and the tobacco companies who continue to exploit the addictive aspects of cigarettes.

Just This One Time

There are times when you know certain personal conduct is wrong, but you do it anyway under a mistaken belief that you are only going to do it this one time and you will never again engage in such conduct. There is a television commercial that promotes a certain brand of potato chips by stating that once you've tasted the chips, you won't be able to eat just one: you'll want the whole bag. This is the problem with the "just this one time" rationalization for unethical conduct. As many of us have learned the hard way, once you've started down a path of misconduct, it is extraordinarily difficult to stop. There is rarely just one occurrence of misconduct. Have you ever told a lie and then had to lie to others in order to protect and preserve the first lie?

Peer Pressure

There is tremendous vulnerability in the human need for acceptance. During our teen years, we were subjected to great pressure to comply with and abide by certain peer perceptions and expectations. Thinking back on those times, didn't you participate in certain behaviors as a result of peer pressure? This need to be liked and accepted never goes away. It may diminish as we individuate and develop greater confidence in ourselves, but the pressure to conform never dies. Peer pressure is often used in the corporate world as a means to motivate an individual. Have you ever been in a situation where you knew you were right, but for the sake of the team or as result of peer pressure, you simply compromised or complied with the expectations of the others in the group?

Self-Deception

When we look in the mirror to examine ourselves, there is a natural human tendency to see only our goodness, strengths, positive features and virtuous personality traits. There is an innate resistance to perceiving our dark side, our weaknesses, negative qualities and deficiencies. This tendency results in an inflated, incomplete and inaccurate perception of ourselves. We mistakenly believe we possess genuine self-awareness, when in reality we do not. Our personal self-deception often keeps us in the dark about our true, genuine and authentic selves. Self-deception also results in ethical blindness—an inability to perceive ourselves and our conduct as being unethical.

My son David taught me a lesson about my own self-deception and blindness. When David was a sophomore in high school, he played football and was a starter on the varsity squad. I was a proud parent as I sat in the stands and watched him perform. After David's first game, I noticed that his pass blocking skills could use improvement. The following day, I spoke to him about this and told him I could help with this skill. I took him out in the yard and told him to rush at me like a defensive lineman. I told him I would demonstrate the proper pass-blocking skills he needed to develop.

He naturally resisted my efforts, smiling and laughing as I urged him to let me show him a few techniques. He told me he could easily hurt me if I persisted. He told me I was an old man, out of shape, and even if I did know something about pass blocking, I learned it a long time ago when football was played under different rules. I did not have these same perceptions, so I would not let him off the hook.

Finally, David resigned himself to the fact that he had

to endure this lesson from his father. He positioned and readied himself. I got down in a three-point stance. I called a snap count and rose up to block him. I was intent on protecting my imaginary quarterback.

I don't remember much after the snap count. I felt a sharp initial pain in my chest and my chin. I recall being sent backward in the air, landing on my tailbone, feeling excruciating pain shooting up through my spine. I recall my back hitting the ground and hearing the breath rush out of my lungs. I lost consciousness when my head whiplashed back onto the ground. All of this occurred in less than two seconds!

When I awoke, David was standing over me, peering into my eyes and laughing so hard tears were running down his face. He muttered something about how silly I looked twitching on the ground and gasping for breath! He helped me up and I never again offered to help him with his pass-blocking techniques or any other aspect of football.

This was a good lesson for me in self-deception. You see, David weighed 210 pounds, was as strong as an ox and physically fit. I, on the other hand, was 42 years old, a bit out of shape, somewhat overweight and getting gray. But for some unknown reason, when I looked in the mirror before going out with David and making a fool of myself, I saw and believed myself to be a physically fit, strong, 18-year-old mass of steel and sex appeal!

This is how insidious self-deception in ethics can be. You can lose total perspective on yourself and never know that you are suffering from ethical blindness.

Changed Circumstances

Often we find ourselves in new circumstances where conditions have changed in unanticipated ways. The changes make keeping promises difficult as illustrated by our Bemidji story.

When the first Gulf War occurred, thousands of young men and woman who had enlisted in the National Guard and in various military reserve units during peaceful times found themselves being activated and called to serve full time in the Middle East. Many voluntarily fulfilled their commitments. A good number reluctantly served while a large number sought to be relieved of their duties claiming "changed circumstances" in their lives. Many of these people claimed family obligations such as young children, spouses or parents in need of support as new conditions in their lives justifying being relieved of their obligations.

Conflicting Duty

Often people find themselves in situations where two or more conflicting duties appear and a choice has to be made as to which duty has priority.

A married friend asks for your help in keeping a secret about his or her romantic fling with another person. Your own spouse suspects that your friend is cheating and asks you if your friend is "stepping out" on his or her spouse. Which duty takes priority? Loyalty to your friend or telling the truth to your own spouse?

As a police officer sworn to uphold the law, do you look the other way when a colleague "roughs up" a suspect who spits on you and your colleague? Do you report this incident which is your duty or do you remain silent out of concern for yourself and your colleague?

Your child wins a competitive four year scholarship to college saving you thousands of dollars. After the first year you inadvertently learn that your child cheated during the scholarship competition by submitting an essay he did not personally write. Which duty has priority? Truth or loyalty?

You want to replace the siding on your house with stucco. You negotiate a great cost savings deal with a contractor. The savings total $10,000.00. This savings is available to you only because the contractor had another party unexpectedly cancel a job that was immediately scheduled to begin, and he can mobilize on your house and get the work done quickly with the same materials that have a limited installation time frame.

You authorize the job without checking with your

spouse. When you tell her that the workmen are coming tomorrow to begin the installation, she emphatically tells you that is not possible since the precious hummingbirds who use the eaves of the house's roof for nesting just had their new baby birds hatched and these new aviary arrivals in the world will be disturbed by the work on your home. She is adamant even when you tell her about the savings. Which duty takes priority? Loyalty to wife? Environmental duty to the humming birds? Promise made to the contractor? Duty to yourself to save money?

What about the end of life scenarios faced by many people with dying family members suffering from incurable diseases, enduring excruciating pain, and who beg you to help them end their lives. Which duty prevails? The legal obligation to refrain from assisting another in committing suicide under threat of being criminally prosecuted for aiding and abetting another in the act of suicide? The duty to treat others with human dignity? The duty to preserve the sanctity of human life? The obligation to treat others with mercy?

When duties, obligations, and interests conflict, something must give. One of the conflicting duties must take priority over the others. Often when a controversial choice is made, other people perceive that choice as being unethical since the competing interest preferred by them was not advanced.

Greed

The relentless pursuit of money, power and fame is a major reason many people engage in unethical conduct. There isn't much I can say to expound on this topic other than that if left unchecked and unbalanced by notions of goodness and virtue, greed, in one of its many forms, will cause unethical conduct.

Relative Pain

An elected official once shared with me that his occasional lapses into unethical conduct occur because he no longer feels the pain of acting unethical. He related most candidly that politics involve compromising one's ethics and values, and that it is such a common experience he no longer feels the pains of guilt or remorse. He related to me that it was like a boxer or football player who simply shrugs off the violent hits that are a necessary part of the job. There is initial great pain, but over time, and relatively speaking, in comparison to other life trauma, the pain of acting unethical becomes nominal. In essence, you become numb to the pain of acting unethically, you get desensitized to the gut wrenching warning signs of impending unethical conduct, and you simply no longer feel your conscience, or a sense of wrong doing.

Unthinking Reflexes

As outlined in previous chapters, each of us is subject and vulnerable to a variety of emotional responses, internalizations and conditioned reflexes. These unthinking, automatic human responses cause much of the unethical conduct we see today. People simply do not pause, think and carefully consider their options before deciding upon a course of conduct. Instead, they too often encounter a dilemma, react emotionally and behave without exercising reflective judgment.

Inability to Control Human Emotions

If you consider all of the foregoing reasons for unethical conduct, you might realize the existence of a common factor—the presence of a strong, underlying, and unchecked human emotion that drives and influences behavior.

Plato is attributed with the Greek conception of the human soul as having three distinct aspects: Pathos, Logos, and Ethos.

Pathos was the label for the aspect of the human soul characterized by unbridled passion, intense feelings, and flaming emotions. Pathos dominated the human soul and resulted in spontaneous, impulsive, behaviors which often were excessive or "over the edge" of human reason.

Logos was that part of the human soul grounded on

logic, reason, thought, calmness, deliberateness and con-templation. Logos was the center of the human intellec-tual experience and served to temper the red hot passions of Pathos.

Logos and Pathos were thought of as being at war with each other—competing for dominance of the human soul. When Pathos and Logos where in balance, it was believed that Ethos—the third component of the human soul emerged. Ethos was characterized by goodness, virtue, and a higher state of being reflecting all that was desirable in the human condition.

When Logos was not sufficient to temper Pathos, or when Pathos·was excessively strong, unethical human conduct was believed to be the end result.

The philosophy of Stoicism with its focus on the sup-pression of emotion as a means of achieving the good and virtuous life was followed by many prominent Greeks and Romans, such as Epictetus and Marcus Aurelius.

The effect of emotion in moral decision making has been observed and documented in many ways. Scientists tell us that we have brain structures which correspond to Logos (neocortex) and Pathos (amygdala). The neocor-tex is the center of reasoning while the amygdala is high-ly correlated with emotions.

Joshua Green, a neuroscientist at Harvard University, explored the effect emotions have on moral decision making. He found evidence supporting the theory that when people personalize a situation, or have a personal stake in the outcome of a moral dilemma, logic based thinking occurs less than emotional based decision making.

In the study, researchers presented subjects with two hypothetical scenarios. In the first, subjects had to decide how to handle a situation where they were forced to turn a switch which would divert a speeding oncoming train to either a course which would eventually cause the death of five workers repairing train tracks, or to a course which would result in the death of a single worker.

Most participants resolved this issue by causing the train to follow the course which killed only one worker and spared the lives of the other five workers. In follow-up interviews most subjects reported their rationale as being it is better to save the lives of five people with only one loss of life, than it is to save one person's life at the expense of five deaths. Most subjects reported that their decision was clearly logic based and was an easy decision to make.

In the second scenario, the hypothetical was changed so that the only choice the subjects faced was to do nothing and let the train proceed to kill five workers, or to push a bystander into the path of the on-coming train. Participants were told that the body mass of the bystander was more than enough to cause the train to stop and save the lives of the five workers. Participants were also told that they could not sacrifice themselves in place of the bystander since their body mass was insufficient to cause the train to stop.

In this situation, the logical choice was once again to save five people at the expense one person—the bystander. But unlike the first scenario, here the majority of participants chose the more deadly option of allowing five people to die by not pushing the bystander into the path of the train.

During the post decision interviews, subjects reported "emotional distress," great uneasiness and anxiety. They further reported that they were reluctant to push the bystander since pushing a person was more "personal" to them than turning a switch. They also reported feeling that they would potentially suffer adverse legal consequences as a result of pushing someone into the train, regardless of the beneficial outcome. Self-concern and doing what was in their best interest was a common theme.

The most interesting finding of the study resulted from reviews of the participants' brain activity recorded during the presentation of the hypotheticals to the subjects and during their deliberations. Each subject underwent a functional MRI during the experiment so that the physical structures of their brains associated with emotion and logic could be monitored during their deliberations.

The MRI results indicated that the brain regions most active in the first scenario were the logic centers while the emotional structures of the brain were less active. In the second scenario, the opposite was discovered. The emotional centers were highly active while the thought centers were quiet.

The key finding of the study was that moral decision making involves either logical thinking or emotional feeling, and those feelings of self-preservation, personal involvement, and other emotional reactions are more likely to overcome pure logic when a person faces a moral crisis.

The pull of human emotions and the natural inclinations for self preservation and self interest are so strong that when activated by an ethical dilemma, it is very difficult to think clearly, and it is nearly impossible to stop the cascading effects of the flood of emotions which naturally occur in such situations.

Psychologists refer to the overwhelming effect of emotion as the "emotional hijack," which metaphorically speaking holds our logic centers hostage for awhile, and delays the start of rational thinking and contemplative judgment.

Several well known celebrity personalities have

experienced public emotional hijacks and revealed the devastating effects of what can happen when we lose control of our emotions. The most notable include: Charlie Sheen (domestic violence charges); Mel Gibson (racial slurs and verbal outrage); Britney Spears (child custody issues); Lindsay Lohan (drugs); and Paris Hilton (drugs and driving while intoxicated). Each celebrity's emotional outbreak was captured in some way by the media and highly publicized. Not a celebrity, but certainly instantaneously famous is Brian Slater, the flight attendant who in 2010 "flipped out" when dealing with an unruly airline passenger, grabbed a beer and exited the aircraft via its emergency chute. Mr. Slater's emotional behavior reminded us that emotional hijacks can happen to normal everyday people as well as celebrities.

There are many reasons why good people act unethically, but the common root of all is the inability to control human passions. Being able to control your emotions and overcome your natural tendency for self-preservation will serve you well in the future. If you can manage your emotions with intelligence you have a better chance of staying on the ethical pathway.

A Few Personal Questions

I'm sure there are many other reasons people engage in

unethical conduct. My list is not a thorough and exhaustive compilation. It represents a starting point to consider in your examination of why you have acted unethically in your life.

I encourage you to examine your own life and reflect a moment on those instances in which you may have been unethical. Think of a time in your life when you acted unethically. Recall the circumstances and the specific factors and challenges you faced.

What motivated you to act the way do did? What were you thinking or feeling at the time? Why did you violate your own ethical standards?

Take the time right now and pause, consider and identify why you took that particular unethical path or made the decision that you or others believed to be unethical. It is in such contemplation that insight, growth and learning about the true nature of your ethics can occur.

Can you identify the causes of your past unethical conduct? What reasons have you used to justify your past misconduct?

CHAPTER 10

What Are Ethical Types?

What are the ethical and moral principles that guide, influence and shape your choices in the ethical dilemmas you encounter? Can you identify, articulate and defend these principles? When you are confronted with an ethical or moral dilemma, what are the fundamental ethical beliefs that you use to resolve the dilemma?

Consider for a moment each of the following ethical situations, make a decision in response to what you read below, and then identify each ethical principle that comes to mind when you deliberate each scenario.

You might write down the principles as you work through the cases. Your written list will be indicators of the nature of your ethical belief system. Your responses will be clues to the criteria you rely upon when faced with ethical decisions.

The Good Samaritan

A gang in your city has been terrorizing people on the

subway. They have robbed, beaten and raped women during their rampages.

During the gang's last escapade, a rider on the subway pulled a gun, shot and killed one of the gang members who had beaten a young woman and was about to rape her. The rider's heroics stopped the rape and allowed others on the subway to move forward with courage to restrain the other gang members until the police arrived.

The press and other subway riders hailed the passenger who came to their aid as a hero. The press labeled him "The Good Samaritan." The community also rallied around the passenger and honored him at a recent public function.

You are the prosecuting attorney for the city and you have just discovered that the Good Samaritan has a felony criminal record, was on parole at the time of the shooting, and subject to a condition that he could not carry a firearm during his parole. There is a criminal statute that makes it a crime for a parolee to carry a gun while on parole. You are up for re-election next month against a popular opponent who says you are weak on crime.

Sworn to uphold the law as the district attorney, what do you do? Risk public scorn and harm to your reputation by charging the Good Samaritan with a crime which would cause immediate incarceration of the hero? Ignore the violation? Bury the case until after the election? What is the right thing to do?

Torture to Save a Colleague

You are a young inexperienced lieutenant in command of an army reserve unit during the first Gulf War. Your mission is to deliver supplies to a front line unit. Your convoy has been ambushed and several of your personnel are seen being dragged away by the enemy. You know they will be tortured and mutilated unless you act quickly to save them.

Your sergeant brings you a captured enemy soldier who refuses to disclose the location of his unit's hiding place and location to which your soldiers have been taken. Time is of the essence. If you do not act immediately most assuredly your friends and colleagues, one of whom is a woman will perish.

Your sergeant urges you to beat the prisoner and to torture him to extract the information needed to save your captured troops. Other soldiers in your unit are urging the same violence. Your sergeant sees your hesitation, and begins to take matters into his own hands.

What would you do? Torture the prisoner yourself? Allow the sergeant to torture the prisoner? Stop the sergeant at the risk of your own unit rebelling against you? Report the sergeant if he tortures? Ignore the situation?

Would you torture the prisoner if one of the taken soldiers from your unit was your son? What does ethics require of you?

Lifeboat Scenario

You are in a life boat in the middle of the north Atlantic. It is February and the conditions are life threatening due to the freezing winds and life robbing cold of the water. You find yourself in this situation after your cruise liner exploded and sank as a result of a terrorist attack. There is room in the life boat for three or four more people.

Hundreds of other survivors are in the water screaming for help. Your life boat is safely floating fifty yards away from the other passengers who are in life vests huddled together in the water without a life boat. You immediately realize those passengers are too weak to swim and will perish if they do not find refuge in a life boat. You try to get others in your life boat to row over and rescue a few of those unfortunate souls.

A large crewman in charge of the life boat ignores your pleas to help the others in the water. He yells at you to sit down or he will throw you overboard. He explains that those in the water will grab the side rails of the boat which will cause the boat to flip over and dump all in the lifeboat into the water. He tells you it is too dangerous to risk. You urge others in the boat to ignore the crewman and to row over and save a few more people who will surely die if you do not act. No one in the life boat will look at you. They glance downward or stare hollow-eyed into the night sky.

What do you do? Pick up an oar and begin to row alone hoping others will see this act of leadership and row with you? Argue and confront the crewman who has a gun? Or will you simply sit down, do nothing and endure the screams of those in the water as they slowly die? What is your ethical responsibility to those in the water? What is the right thing to do?

Custodial Body Cavity Search

You are the Chief of Police of a midsize city in the United States. Your department has a standard policy requiring that suspects of violent crimes, including those who physically assault fellow police officers, are to be strip searched when jailed. The strip search procedure includes an invasive "body cavity" search for contraband. The body cavity search procedure is unpleasant to endure, can be painful at times, and is personally humiliating.

There has been much debate within the police department about the ethics of the body cavity procedure. The lines are clearly drawn between those who see the procedure as necessary and those who feel it is unreasonable and ought to be abandoned in most instances.

Late one evening you receive a call from the shift commander at the jail. He tells you a highly combative woman in her mid 70s assaulted one of your officers by firing a hand gun at him during a domestic violence disturbance. The shift commander wants to know if she is to follow procedure and conduct the standard body cavity procedure on this suspect.

Normally, you would not receive such calls since most perpetrators of domestic violence are men and your jail officers are not bothered by conducting such searches on men. Here the suspect of the crime who shot and injured one of your officers is an elderly woman. Your shift commander wanted to check with you to be sure the strip search policy, including the body cavity procedure was to be followed in this situation. You hear in the background the loud voices of other officers who are upset that a colleague has been shot and are asking why the shift commander is even asking about the policy.

What do you tell the shift commander? Follow the policy? Ignore the policy? Tell her to use her own judgment and let her face the criticism from her fellow officers who want the policy followed without regard to gender? What is the ethical thing to do?

What would you say if you found out the real reason

for the call to you was that the suspect was your mother who was in the early stages of dementia? What if the suspect was in her early twenties and was your daughter who was involved with an abusive spouse? Do these factors change your view of the ethics of body cavity searches? Should these personal factors even enter into your decision concerning what is and is not ethical?

Other Scenarios

Your wife asks you if she looks "fat" in her new jeans. Truthfully, she does, but what are you going to say?

Your elderly dying mother worked for many weeks knitting a sweater as a Christmas gift for your teenage daughter who is highly fashion conscious and brutally candid in her opinions about what clothes look good and what clothes look terrible.

The sweater is a hideous looking orange and purple colored fashion disaster. Your mom lovingly asks your daughter if she likes it, and if she will wear it to school when you she goes back to classes after the Christmas holidays. Your daughter looks at you with a puzzled look for guidance.

What do you do? Intervene and say something to smooth it over knowing your daughter will speak negatively about the sweater? Shake your head in a negative manner indicating to your daughter she better not speak her mind and tell the truth? Hold your breath and let things occur naturally? If the sweater was a gift to you and you would never wear it in public, would you lie to your mom about wearing it?

You are a physician treating a dying patient who needs a medical procedure which he is stubbornly refusing to authorize since he is unreasonably afraid of surgery and the possibility of being in a long term coma as an adverse side effect of the anesthesia.

The procedure you recommend would cure the patient and save his life. The possibility of something going wrong during the procedure is less than 1% which does include the possibility of a long term coma.

You know that the patient will refuse any course of action that even remotely could result in a coma. You know the patient will die within twenty-four hours if he does not have the recommended surgery.

Would you neglect to mention the extremely remote risk of the coma in order to get your patient's consent to the procedure and to save his life, particularly if no one would find out? What if the patient was your son?

A criminal suspect is being transported to jail by you and a fellow police officer who is your best friend. The suspect is verbally abusive to both of you, resists arrest and has to be physically restrained and force must be used to control the suspect.

The suspect spits in your face, head butts you, and then bites you on the arm. Your partner sees this happening and beats the suspects in a fit of rage. Your partner clearly was trying to help you, but was so emotionally overtaken that he actually lost control and used excessive force. The injuries to the suspect require a visit to the hospital. Your partner looks at you and says: "Looks like our suspect accidentally fell down the stairs, don't you agree?" What would you do? Go along with your partner's version of the story since there were no other witnesses? Tell the truth and get your partner in trouble?

You do something extremely stupid like have an affair with a co-worker while on a business trip. It was clearly a mistake, something totally out of character for you, a one time thing which is never likely to happen again. You feel extraordinary guilty. You are highly remorseful. You are ashamed of yourself. You love your spouse dearly. What do you do? Do you tell your spouse what happened?

During negotiations in a business deal, do you tell the truth about your underlying needs and interests? Do you purposefully hold back information from your opponent? Do you intentionally make statements to mislead and misdirect your opponent's thinking about your true intentions and goals? Do you tell your opponent that your most recent offer was your final and best offer when you know this is not true? Do you overstate your options and alternatives in order to get your opponent to accept your offer?

You have inside information that your office will be shutting down operations in six months. You are told that you cannot disclose this information to anyone. Your best friend who is not a high level executive asks you if the office is going to be closed in the near future. What do you say? What are your duties to your friend? Should you be honest? What are your duties to your employer? What is the right thing to do?

If you are overcharged at a checkout counter at the grocery store, do you speak up? If you are undercharged, do you speak up? If you get too much change, do you speak up? What if the clerk shorts you on change, do you speak up?

If you have to choose between one of two equally qualified people for a significant promotion in your company, and one of the candidates is your long time best friend, whom do you promote? Your best friend who can easily do the job, or do you choose the other equally qualified candidate? What duty do you owe your friend? What duty do you owe the other candidate? What duty do you owe your company? What is the right thing to do?

You agree to do go out with a friend for dinner, but you get a better offer for the same time. You would rather accept the better offer. Do you cancel with your friend?

Do you tell your friend the real reason for cancelling? Do you tell a little 'white lie" to avoid hurting her feelings? What do you do?

You are going to take a long, overseas flight to China. You know how uncomfortable the airline seats are so you buy one of those "extra leg room" seats in the economy section of the plane. While getting situated in your seat a flight attendant is assisting a seeing impaired person with a guide dog. The flight attendant approaches you and in front of all of the other passengers, the flight attendant asks you if you would mind trading seats with the seeing impaired person so the seeing eye dog can be more comfortably accommodated in your "extra leg room" seat. You look around and see that there are no other "extra leg room" seats available. In that moment, what do you feel? What do you say or do? What is the ethical thing to do?

You are a cashier at a busy retail outlet. The company policy is that you are responsible for any errors you make and must make up for any shortages in cash which may appear when you reconcile receipts and cash. On many days you find yourself short and having to go into your pocket to pay the difference. You suspect that the starting cash balance is off on those days, but your supervisor consistently shrugs you off. You figure that over the year you have paid close to $500.00 to make things right.

One day as you reconcile your cash at the end of the

day you discover that the cash is more than it should be by about $25.00. Should you pocket the extra money to make up for all the other times when you have had to go into your own purse to make things right? You fear you will you get in trouble if you report excess cash since your supervisor will think you shorted a customer. What is the ethical thing to do? What are you inclined to do at this moment?

You are a newly commissioned second lieutenant in the United States army. Your company commander tells you to do an inspection of the heavy equipment and report back to the commander with a report certifying combat readiness of the equipment. You do your job and find that only 60% of the equipment is combat ready. You advise your company commander of your findings. He is clearly upset and tells you that you must be mistaken and to recheck your work. He tells you that the minimum acceptable requirement is 85% and to make sure that your final report meets the requirement.

You recheck your work and confirm your original findings. Your sergeant, a veteran of many war campaigns, tells you not to worry, fill out the report showing 85% compliance, and everything will be just fine. He tells you that he can get things ready before next week's deployment. One of the other lieutenants who has been with the company longer than you overhears the exchange and tells you that you better do as the sergeant suggests since the company commander will not tolerate officers who cannot get things done his way. What would you do?

You have new neighbors who have just moved in next door to you. They have a mean, vicious pit bull who barks constantly at all hours of the day and night. On several occasions, the dog has tunneled under the fence between your house and your neighbor's house, come into your yard and frightened your children. You tried talking to your neighbor, but he was defensive and hostile toward you. You called the police and the responding officer said the police could do nothing until the dog actually bit someone or was caught in the act of being in your yard. Other neighbors are as frightened and frustrated as you.

Late one night while the dog owners were away from home, you witnessed another neighbor toss several pieces of juicy looking meat scraps over the fence into the pit bulls yard. The next day you learn the dog unexpectedly died. There is a rumor that the pit bull owner is going to move away. A few days later a police officer comes to your house asking if you might have seen anything suspicious during the last week. Do you mention the event you witnessed, or do you remain silent, thankful for the protective remedial actions of your other neighbor? What is the right thing to do?

A dying friend who is suffering horribly from a debilitating, incurable disease asks for help in committing assisted suicide. You see the excruciating pain and suffering of your dear friend. The physicians are unable to manage the pain and your friend is destined to suffer for at least another two months as he continues to deteriorate.

It is a felony in your state to assist another in the commission of a suicide. All your friend asks of you is that you go to his house, pick up his hand gun and bring it to him. No one else hears his daily requests of you. You know you could help him and not leave any evidence of your involvement. Would you help a friend under these circumstances? What if it was someone you loved dearly? Is it really wrong for you to help out in such a way?

Woodpeckers are driving you crazy at your home. They are destroying the cedar siding. They peck on your chimney and the sound is deafening as it travels down the metallic chute and reverberates throughout your house. Wildlife officials are not helpful. They tell you to put up a wooden owl on your roof to deter the woodpeckers. You do so but the offending birds take no notice of the owl. You are at your wits end. Your spouse tells you to just deal with it and to do the repairs each year.

A friend offers to help you out with the problem by coming over with his arsenal of small arms, bows and arrows, and sling shots. Your wife who is an animal lover is going out of town for a few days. You are confident you and your friend could solve the problem of the woodpeckers without getting caught by your wife or being seen by neighbors who might be offended. Would you proceed to eliminate the problem in the manner suggested by your friend? Over the last three years, you have spent close to $7,500.00 making annual repairs to your home as a result of the woodpeckers. What is the right thing to do?

You coach a high school basketball team in an important playoff game. The score is tied with less than ten seconds remaining in the game. The official has just ruled that your team is entitled to possession of the ball. The official believes one of the opposing players was the last to touch the ball as it bounced out of bounds.

The incident happened directly in front of you and you clearly saw the ball glance off your player's left foot after being touched by the other player. You know the official made a mistake. Your home team fans are cheering about the call while the opposing team's fans are yelling that the official made a mistake. Your player whose foot the ball touched going out of bounds looks at you with a facial expression of guilt. Whoever gets possession will have a definite advantage in the waning seconds of the game. What is the right thing to do? Correct the mistake of the official? Say nothing? What would you do?

Ethical Principles

As you read each of the above described scenarios, did you experience conflicting notions of right and wrong? Did you perceive uneasiness or hesitation in deciding the right course of action? Did you rely upon certain ethical principles or values in your deliberations? Did you actually use your ethical principles? If so, which principles came to mind? What was the basis of each decision? As a result of your experience with each scenario, can you now draw any conclusions about the nature of your ethics? Most important, what do your responses to the scenarios say or reveal about your ethics?

Ethical Types

Over the years I have asked people to explain to me the architecture of their ethical belief systems. I have probed in focus groups for the underlying ethical principles people rely upon when confronted with ethically challenging situations. I have researched the philosophical literature in an effort to capture and understand the great moral principles that guide ethical decisions.

As a result of my investigations, I learned that there are seven primary ways in which people approach ethics. I have learned that there are seven distinct ethical styles or ethical personalities.

These differential approaches to ethics represent

seven ethical typologies or preferences to personal decision making during an ethical or moral crisis. I refer to these approaches as Ethical Types.

Do you know your personal ethical preferences? Do you know your ethical type? Can you identify, articulate and defend your ethical type?

The seven preferences or ethical types are Egoism, Utilitarianism, Existentialism, Divine Command, Deontology, Conformism and Eclectic.

Egoism

Egoism's central and fundamental principle is that when you are confronted by an ethical dilemma, the right thing to do is to choose or undertake that action which is in your self-interests. Egoism is that inner drive that compels you to seek, maximize and promote the greatest good for yourself. It is a results-oriented preference that causes you to analyze the possible consequences under a variety of options, and then select the alternative which will be best for you.

When you focus on yourself, without regard for the consequences others may experience, your spiritual principles, the duties and obligations you owe to others and how other feel about your decision, you have adopted Egoism as your primary ethical type.

Although Egoism has, for many individuals, a negative

emotional aura, it has been the underlying basis of the free market enterprise system. Egoism was promoted by Adam Smith, the most popular of the free market enterprise believers. Smith wrote that if each person in a society pursued his or her own self-interests, this focus on self would results in the fairest and most efficient distribution of goods, services and wealth.

People who are highly influenced by Egoism tend to be survivors, analytical and acutely aware of the consequences and implications of their conduct. Because the ethical choices of those who embrace Egoism do not always take into account the needs of others, their self-interested choices often result in harsh consequences for the rest of the world. At times, this self-centeredness can make family, business and social relationships difficult to maintain.

Egoism occurs a great deal in our society. We see it a lot in business, entertainment and sports, where highly paid executives, entertainers and athletes with egoism as the basis of their decisions, sell themselves to the highest bidders in order to achieve financial greatness and independence.

Many people fail to recognize that egoism is a natural and strong determinant of their human behavior. For some reason we have difficulty seeing this part of ourselves. It is easier for us to recognize it in others, but harder to see as a part of our ethical beliefs.

Gandhi was once asked if his reason for living and working within an impoverished village was to help others, and to advance humanitarian interests. Ghandi, the epitome of self-sacrifice, insightfully replied that he was in the village to serve no one else but himself, to find his own self-realization by serving others. Gandhi's reply serves to remind us that our self interest is a huge factor when it comes to deciding what is right and wrong. For some reason we have a hard time consciously recognizing it.

There are certainly times when Egoism is justified—when your life is threatened or when others will not be harmed by your conduct. There are other occasions when it certainly raises cause for concern.

To what extent do you prefer and demonstrate Egoism in your ethical decisions? What decision or course of conduct have you recently undertaken that was purely in your self-interest? How often do you do so?

Utilitarianism

Utilitarianism is associated with the historical writings of Jeremy Bentham and John Stuart Mill. Its central and fundamental principle is that one should, when resolving ethical dilemmas, choose the path that is in the collective best interests of the greatest number of people.

Utilitarianism requires you to seek the greatest good for the greatest number of people.

Like Egoism, Utilitarianism is a results-oriented preference. If you are influenced by this moral preference, you look at the consequences of your action in relation to how it will affect others. Unlike Egoism's focus on self, Utilitarianism focuses on the welfare of others. This is done without regard for the eventual consequences to self, spiritual principles, your sense of duty, or how others may feel about the decision you make.

The Utilitarian preference does not easily accommodate minority views and interests. It often results in consequences that are harsh and sometimes harmful to those whose needs and interests do not coincide with the greater good. The impact of a Utilitarian decision falls disproportionately upon a small group of individuals whose needs will be sacrificed so that the larger population will benefit.

To what extent do you use Utilitarianism in your moral decision making? How often do you sacrifice your self-interests, or the interests of the minority in order to advance the needs and interests of others?

Existentialism

Existentialism was made popular by the writings of Soren Kierkegaard, Jean Paul Sartre and Albert Camus.

Existentialism's central principle is that when confronted with an ethical dilemma, you should look within yourself for the right moral path to follow, and that you should make a conscious choice to follow your deeper, inner sense of what is right and wrong. If you feel a strong drive to act in accordance with what you believe to be the inner purity of your heart, or if you feel compelled to "be true to yourself," then you are heavily influenced by Existentialism.

Existentialism is an ethical preference that is evidenced by a need and desire to focus on how you feel and the nature of your inner state of being. This preference is grounded upon human autonomy and the conscious exercise of free will. Although a person who is heavily influenced by Existentialism may consider external consequences, spiritual principles, duties, or the influence of others in the deliberation of what is right or wrong, the ultimate deciding factor will be the person's inner, intuitive feeling of right and wrong.

One of the challenges of Existentialism is that human internalizations, such as personal biases, prejudices, emotions, thoughts, denials and deceptions, make it very difficult to discover and express the authentic inner purity of the human heart.

To what extent are you influenced by Existentialism? Does your personal conduct reflect your inner purity?

Divine Command

Divine Command or Divine Inspiration, as it is sometimes referred to, is an ethical preference evident in the belief that when confronted by an ethical dilemma, you should follow the word of God, as reflected in scripture, religious doctrines or spiritual teachings. It is based upon the principle that God's will must be obeyed, and that you should subordinate human desires and temptations to God's laws.

Divine Command is not limited to a particular religious sect or denomination. It encompasses all religious beliefs: Christian, Jewish, Islamic, Buddhist, Hindu, Taoist, Catholic, etc. Regardless of your individual religious affiliation, if you look to God's word to resolve ethical dilemmas, then you are heavily influenced by Divine Command.

The Divine Command preference provides clear and straightforward answers to ethical dilemmas for those who are influenced by it. They tend to accept God's word, act accordingly, and expect others to do the same.

There is great diversity of belief across the religious spectrum. This sometimes makes it difficult to discover, interpret and consistently follow God's word. At times, God's word is misinterpreted by man and is used as an instrument of evil by misguided and disturbed individuals.

Is Divine Command an important and relevant influence in your ethical decision making?

Deontology

Deontology's central and fundamental principle is that ethical dilemmas are best resolved by following certain prescribed duties or obligations that exist or are imposed by virtue of a person's existence as a human being, in affiliation with a cultural, societal, professional, business, or other trade group or occupation.

Deontology is a preference grounded upon the belief that ethical dilemmas are best resolved by following the established rules, codes of conduct and duties prescribed by a recognized authority. When confronted with an ethical dilemma, a person influenced by Deontology will search for an applicable or governing duty or obligation, and once it's identified, act in accordance with it. Consequently, external consequences to self or others, personal feelings, spiritual principles and the influence of others are not relevant factors in determining the right thing to do.

Most cultures, societies, professions, organizations, industry groups and businesses have developed elaborate codes of conduct that their members are expected to follow. These prescriptions offer clear-cut answers and outline sanctions for violations.

Some philosophical writers have developed specific duties that they advocate as core human duties and responsibilities owed to other humans. These duties typically include the following: Keep promises. Do no harm to others. Help others. Act reasonably and prudently in relation to others. Pay for your mistakes. Take care of your family. Do not lie, cheat, or steal.

During one of my visits to the National Archives in Washington, D.C., I discovered a book that embodied the spirit and essence of deontology. It was a book written by George Washington which outlined 110 rules for civilized conduct. The rules were simple and straight forward. They covered a variety of dos and don'ts.

One of the more amusing rules I discovered was the admonishment by Washington to never speak while chewing meat in your mouth! My favorite rule which I found most meaningful was Rule 110 which urged that a person should always strive to keep alive in their breast, the celestial fire known as "thy conscience."

Many rules and duties are taught to us by our parents during our childhood. I am sure that many of us can easily recall our parents' admonishments to share, tell the truth, say you are sorry, do not do steal, etc.

One of my favorite lists of duties came to me from my involvement with the Boy Scouts. As a young scout I learned that a Boy Scout is: trustworthy, loyal, helpful, friendly, courteous, kind, obedient, cheerful, thrifty, brave, clean and reverent. Additionally, a Boy Scout is expected to "do a good deed daily."

To what extent are you influenced by Deontology? What duties and responsibilities do you believe you owe to others? What rules echo in your mind from time to time?

Conformism or Social Relevance

Conformism's central and fundamental principle is that when confronted with an ethical dilemma, a person ought to look to family, friends, colleagues, or a relevant social peer group and undertake an action, or resolve the dilemma in a manner consistent with the perceived values and expectations of that group.

Conformism is also known as the Principle of Social Relevance and Social Acceptance. It is the notion that if you do not adhere to the social expectations and norms of society, you will be ostracized and excluded from membership in society. Social Relevance is a strong underlying group pressure to conform.

A person who is influenced by Conformism will avoid decisions and actions that conflict with the expectations of the relevant peer group. Peer pressure, the inherent human need to be accepted as a member of a group, concern for what others will think, and the need to avoid criticism and ridicule are concerns for a person who follows Conformism.

Adolescents are particularly vulnerable to this preference. I am sure you can recall times during this stage of your life when you felt the pressures to be like others, and you did things which were not natural to you but which you did because of the social need for acceptance.

Over the years, I have watched with amusement as my children have gone through their adolescent years and been influenced by their peer groups. I have seen my children change how they dress so they can be more like others at school. I have watched in wonder and despair as one of my daughters pierced her body in places I would have never imagined as being suitable for piercing—all in an effort so she could wear rings, posts, stubs, etc. like her friends at school. I have also watched as my children have colored, cut, and at times, not cut their hair in certain styles in order to more closely identify with their peers. I have even had two of my children use their bodies as art mediums for various tattoo "artists." All of this behavior was driven by adolescent pressures to belong, to be a part of a group.

Conformism keeps you close to societal norms if your relevant peer group is sufficiently broad and representative of society at large. However, Conformism can and often does interfere with individual reflective judgment.

It can also result in adverse consequences when the relevant peer group's influence is too strong or misaligned with society at large. Gang behavior, mob behavior, religious group suicide cults, and racial and gender hate groups are extreme examples of what can happen with this ethical type.

Eclectic

The Eclectic ethical preference is one that blends and relies upon two or more of the previously described ethical types. It results from the competing influences of the various ethical preferences you may experience. Thus, when confronted with an ethical dilemma, the Eclectic preference will take into account the influence of each preference and refrain from relying solely upon one of them as the guiding basis of behavior.

If you prefer to gather information and deliberate about an ethical decision by looking at how your decision will affect you, how it will affect others, how you will feel about it, whether or not your decision will reflect your genuine self, how God's word might guide your decision, whether or not you have certain duties you must fulfill and how others will view your decision, you are probably strongly influenced by the Eclectic preference.

The competing influences for a person who is an Eclectic often cause ethical decision-making to be an agonizing and difficult process. On occasion, a person who is influenced by the Eclectic preference will appear to act inconsistently with prior decisions and conduct.

To what extent do you rely upon several ethical preferences in resolving your ethical dilemmas? Are you an Eclectic?

Discovering Your Ethical Type

Egoism, Utilitarianism, Existentialism, Divine Command, Deontology, Conformism and Eclectic represent seven different ways of resolving moral dilemmas. Each person has a preferred way of resolving ethical dilemmas. This primary preference is referred to as your "ethical type."

You are influenced, to some extent, by each of the ethical types. But if you honestly examine your past conduct, you should be able to determine which of the seven ethical preferences has most influenced your personal conduct, as well as the extent to which you are influenced by secondary ethical types.

Take a moment now and do this. Recall a time when you faced a difficult ethical decision. What did you do? What ethical preference was the basis of your conduct at that time?

Did you focus on what was best for you? Were you concerned with what might be best for others? Did you go within to find your inner purity and act in a way that was reflective of this inner state of being? Did you look to God for inspiration? Did you fulfill your duties and obligations? Did you conform your conduct to the expectations of others? Did you seek to incorporate the ethical prescriptions of several different types? Review your responses to each of the ethical scenarios outlined earlier in this chapter. Can you identify any of the seven ethical types as the basis for your choices?

Can you now identify your primary ethical type? Can you identify the extent to which you are influenced by other secondary ethical types?

If you are interested in exploring your personal ethical makeup in greater depth, you should consider taking The Ethical Type Indicator, a personal assessment instrument that reveals a person's ethical preferences. The instrument is available at www.EthicalTypeIndicator.com and www.LouieLarimer.com.

Additional Self-Discovery

Knowing your ethical type or ethical preference is a good starting point for additional self-discovery.

Ask yourself the following questions:

- Is your stated ethical type truly reflective of the way you resolve ethical dilemmas?
- Should you continue to rely upon this ethical preference?

- Can you articulate why you prefer this ethical type?

- Do any of the other ethical types have merit or value?

- Do any of the other ethical types appeal to you?

- Are there situations in which one of the other ethical types might be more appropriate?

- Can you rank how the secondary ethical types influence your personal conduct?

Understanding Others

Once you have achieved an understanding of your own ethical type, you can use the ethical typology to gain an understanding and appreciation of how others resolve, justify and defend their ethical positions.

If you develop an appreciation of each ethical type, and if during an ethical discussion you listen carefully to what is being said, you will soon be able to recognize the underlying ethical types others rely upon. This insight will give you a deeper understanding of others' ethical constitutions and why they hold certain beliefs. This awareness will also help you to understand that human belief systems are as diverse as race, gender, age and religion. Hopefully, this knowledge will help you develop a greater tolerance of opposing views.

You can begin to enhance your understanding of others by doing the following:

- Telling others about the seven ethical types.

- Sharing with them your primary ethical type and secondary preferences.

- Asking your spouse, children, family, friends and colleagues to characterize how they perceive your ethical type.

- Listening carefully to others as they speak. Observe their behavior for clues as to their ethical preferences.

- Making inquiries and asking questions of others to identify and explain the ethical or moral basis for their choices and personal conduct.

A Tool Of Communication

Knowing the seven ethical types can also help you communicate, persuade and influence others in a powerful and effective way. If you are engaged in a discussion in which you are attempting to persuade a colleague to adopt a particular view on an issue, your chances of success are increased and enhanced if you know your colleague's ethical type.

Have you ever attempted to persuade another person to adopt your ethical perspective on an issue by bombarding them with facts, figures, analysis and arguments that are grounded upon your own ethical beliefs and preferences? Didn't you become frustrated when your arguments failed to persuade this person to accept your ethical position?

Your failure should not be surprising. It should be understandable when you realize that not everyone shares your ethical type and preference. You should recognize that if the other person's ethical type is different from yours, this person will most likely derive a substantially different conclusion from yours.

Remember that Utilitarianism is incompatible with Egoism. Existentialism is substantially different from Deontology, Conformism and Divine Command. In essence, your arguments amount to being a round peg in a square hole. To be successful, you must know the other person's ethical type and present ethical arguments based upon his or her ethical preferences, not yours. In other words, you must shape the peg to fit into the other person's square. You do this by knowing what each ethical type requires, knowing the person's ethical type, and then creating arguments consistent that person's ethical type to support your ethical conclusion. If you do this, you will find greater success in communicating and influencing others.

CHAPTER 11

What is a Core Ethical Value?

I recently read a short biography of Benjamin Franklin. I learned that Franklin was born in 1706. He was the tenth son and fifteenth child of a Boston soap and candle maker. When he was twelve years old, he became an indentured apprentice to his brother. He spent five years learning the printing business. When he was 17, he left Boston and journeyed to New York. He found no work there and so resumed a long and arduous journey that took him to Philadelphia.

He arrived in Philadelphia with two shillings, a few tattered clothes and four rolls of bread. He spent five years in youthful indulgence, but gradually emerged from this experience with a remarkable entrepreneurial talent. He ultimately established his own printing business, took over the bankrupt Pennsylvania Gazette and published Poor Richard's Almanac.

He served as clerk to the Pennsylvania Assembly until

his own election as a representative. He also served as postmaster of Philadelphia. When Franklin was 42, he left business and embarked on a series of remarkable public ventures. His public accomplishments included: establishing the first public subscription library, organizing Pennsylvania's first militia and helping to create Philadelphia's first city watch, fire company, college, hospital and fire insurance company. He served as grand master of Pennsylvania's Freemasons and founded the American Philosophical Society. He took an active part in encouraging the paving and lighting of Philadelphia's streets.

Franklin also pioneered the development of what is now known as a "networking" group. He established a club devoted to mutual improvement. The club required each member to profess a love for mankind and truth. Additionally, it required each member to take turns writing and presenting views on points of morality, politics, or natural philosophy. The group was devoted to mixing the business of doing good with the business of getting ahead. It did this by cultivating and utilizing professional and business connections.

The most impressive aspect of Franklin's life, in my view, was his personal project to "arrive at moral perfection." Remarkably, at age 25, Franklin developed a list of thirteen virtues that he felt were desirable or necessary in order to achieve moral perfection. Franklin's virtues were temperance, silence, order, resolution, frugality, industry, sincerity, justice, moderation, cleanliness, tranquility, chastity and humility.

Franklin's list of virtues, though impressive, is not as significant as Franklin's disciplined approach to learning and reflecting the values in his life.

Franklin created a book in which he charted his daily progress toward moral perfection. His system was simple. He allotted a page for each virtue. On each page he created seven columns, one for each day of the week. These columns were crossed by thirteen lines, one for of each of Franklin's virtues. At the end of each day, Franklin would reflect back and mark a little black spot for every fault he committed with respect to each virtue. In this way, Franklin maintained a written moral ledger of his progress.

Much is being written today about virtues and values and the need to incorporate ethical values into our business and professional lives. This resurgence is nothing but a reincarnation of Franklin's thirteen virtues. Many experts, such as Stephen Covey, tout the importance of knowing and behaving in accordance with certain core ethical values or virtues. To my knowledge, none of these "values" or "virtue" experts have undertaken the discipline and effort reflected in Franklin's moral ledger.

Core ethical values are important in making ethical decisions and living a virtuous life. They are those deeply held beliefs that you hold near and dear to your heart. They are concepts and principles that you treasure, value and firmly embrace. Core ethical values are like beacons in the night, which guide you along your desired moral path during turbulent times and in periods of moral ambiguity and ethical confusion.

Core ethical values include such concepts as: loyalty, truth, honesty, respect, trust, friendship, family, fairness, equality, autonomy, freedom, courage, bravery, humility, health, kindness, happiness and education. The list is endless. It is limited only by your imagination and by your choices of what is important.

Do you know your core ethical values or virtues? Have you embarked on a personal journey to moral perfection? Have you developed your personal list of desirable virtues? What virtues are on the list? More importantly, is your conduct or behavior consistent with those virtues? Do you walk your own talk? What would your moral ledger reflect?

Core Values

The answers to the following questions will help you identify your core ethical values and the virtues that are important to you:

- Where and how do you spend your time?
- On what do you spend your money?
- What is truly important to you?
- How have you reacted to critical incidents or crises in your life?
- How have you treated other people during such times of crisis?
- What will others say about your core ethical values?

Ask others if your behavior reflects the values you have just written. Be open to the process. Include your family, employees, friends and customers in the inquiry. If you have the discipline, chart your progress in your own moral ledger.

From an organizational standpoint, develop a list of ethical values to guide the business behavior of your employees. Tell them your business philosophy and ethical expectations. Remind them frequently of these values. More importantly, demonstrate and reflect these values in your own conduct. Your employees may not listen to what you say, but they will critically examine your behavior and conduct.

Benjamin Franklin is known to have said: "The way to wealth is as plain as the way to market. It depends chiefly on two words, industry and frugality. He who gets all he can honestly and saves all he gets will certainly become rich."

Franklin's successful private entrepreneurship and his public accomplishments clearly demonstrate that he walked his own talk. Will others say as much about you?

Part II

THE SEVEN STEPS

Doing
the right thing
requires a lot of a person.

CHAPTER 12

Ethical Virtuosity

Ethical Virtuosity refers to a person's ability to consistently identify, confront and resolve ethical dilemmas in a manner that reflects goodness. It is demonstrated by personal conduct that is noble, honorable and virtuous in all respects. In other words, it is consistently doing the right thing, at the right time.

How do you achieve ethical virtuosity? What must you do to be able to consistently do the right thing at the right time?

I believe there are seven basic steps you need to take if you want to achieve ethical virtuosity.

First, you must look inward and discover a few things about yourself. This involves critically examining who you are, what you believe in, and what is truly important to you.

Second, you must search for, study and evaluate the body of ethical knowledge that has been left to us by the great philosophers. This requires special effort, since the moral legacy of the great philosophers is a bit challenging to comprehend and apply in today's fast-paced, rapidly changing world of technology.

Third, you must develop a relevant, comprehensive and meaningful ethical belief system. This requires that you identify, determine, choose and develop, your life's mission, personal beliefs and core ethical values.

Fourth, you must learn and practice emotional discipline. This requires you to master your internalizations and other factors that get in the way of your achieving ethical virtuosity.

Fifth, you must consciously exercise, on a moment by moment basis, your individual human autonomy (your free will) to conform and align your behavior to your ethical belief system.

Sixth, you must demonstrate moral courage and personal accountability on a daily basis. This requires you to know what each of these principles requires of you as a human being.

Seventh, you must develop an individual action plan that contains specific behavioral goals, personal commitments and an evaluation system to track your progress.

If you undertake, complete and practice the seven steps just outlined, you can achieve ethical virtuosity and come close to the moral perfection that Benjamin Franklin and others have sought throughout history.

CHAPTER 13

Step 1: Develop Self-Awareness

Socrates is known to have said: "Know thyself." He also said: "The unexamined life is not worth living."

Both of these ancient platitudes, though concise in form and simple in statement, reveal the first step toward achieving ethical virtuosity—engaging in a process of self-assessment that leads to self-knowledge.

This first step involves critical self-examination, personal insight and authentic self-awareness. It requires getting in touch with your genuine inner core, knowing what you believe in, and understanding your personal psychology of ethics.

People who know themselves are able to articulate what is truly important in their lives. They have a strong sense of purpose in life. They know their core ethical values. They can easily relate and defend the ethical principles that guide their lives. They know their ethical type. They are able to define what ethics, integrity and good moral character mean in their lives. They know their personal failings and are able to identify those occasions when their behavior conflicts with their ethical values. They know why they have acted unethically in the past. They know the extent to which their ethical beliefs are shaped and influenced by parents, friends, and media, past experience, education, culture, internalizations, conditioned reflexes and reflective judgment. They know their preferred defense mechanisms and how these rationalizations, projections and denials interfere with their ethical decision making. They have a genuine knowledge of their authentic self.

Do you know as much about yourself? Can you relate the same information concerning your ethical constitution? More importantly, will you take the time to do the work that will allow you to genuinely know the essence of your ethical core? If you have reflected upon and answered the questions I have presented throughout this work, you will find yourself remarkably insightful concerning your ethical state of being. If you have not done this work, I can only urge that you revisit these questions and complete these important exercises.

Becoming self-aware involves much more than the ethical inquiries I have presented thus far. The process of self-discovery goes beyond your ethical personality. Here are some of the other areas of inquiry you ought to undertake as a means of connecting with yourself.

Do you have a strong sense of your purpose and meaning in this life? What is that purpose? Have you captured the purpose in a written statement of your life's mission? Will you do so now?

What is the general condition of your life? Are you genuinely happy? Do you feel passion and excitement in your personal relationships and in your professional work? What is the source of the joy you experience in your life? What sadness and disappointments are you experiencing? What is the true source of this sorrow?

Is your life balanced? Do you spend quality time fulfilling your family obligations, spiritual yearnings, physical and health needs, professional obligations and community responsibilities? Are you neglecting one or more of these fundamental dimensions in your life?

What motivates you? What are the things you would like to do in your life that you have not yet been able to do? What is really keeping you from doing these things?

What are your hopes and dreams? Do you have a vision of an uplifting and positive future? Are you actively working to bring about your hopes, dreams and visions, or have you given up? What obstacles and challenges are preventing you from realizing your future? Are you willing to make the personal sacrifices to create your future? Are you willing to change?

Who are you? What are your strengths? What are your

weaknesses? Are you working to overcome your weaknesses? What are your unique gifts and talents? Are you using these talents in a constructive manner? What are your vulnerabilities? What are your bad habits that you need to change? Do you know how you sabotage or get in the way of your own success?

What do you stand for? How do you define yourself? What is truly important to you? What do you believe in? What do you feel most strongly about in your life? What do you cherish and value?

What do others say about you? How do they perceive you? How will you be remembered? What legacies will you leave behind? Do you genuinely walk your talk? Where have you not done so?

What mistakes have you made in your life? What have you learned from these events?

Are your personal relationships fulfilling and meaningful? Do you need to make changes? How can you improve and enhance your relationships?

What are you missing in your life? What voids do you experience? What are you willing to do about it?

These are just a few of the fundamental life questions you need to address as you strive toward ethical virtuosity. Spend quality time reflecting upon these matters. Your answers will provide valuable and powerful insights.

CHAPTER 14

Step 2:
Seek Ethical Knowledge

The second step toward Ethical Virtuosity involves searching for, studying and acquiring ethical knowledge. The great moral philosophers have left us a vast and rich body of ethical writings and insights. For example, the ancient Greek philosophies of Socrates, Plato, Aristotle, Epictetus and others are still relevant today. The teachings of Jesus, Martin Luther, Thomas Aquinas, Thomas Merton, St. Augustine and others are relied upon by millions of Christians as a way of finding God and living a moral life. The teachings and sayings of Lao Tzu, Buddha and Confucius are followed by millions in the Asian world. There is not a day that goes by without someone quoting Benjamin Franklin, Soren Kierkegaard, John Stuart Mills, Thomas Hobbes and Jean Paul Sartre, to name but a few.

If you want to achieve ethical virtuosity, you must cultivate an intellectual thirst for the insights of the great moral philosophers. You need to read and study the classical writings on ethics. You need to seek out and evaluate newly emerging ethical thought.

The ethical knowledge you gain as a result of your study of the moral legacy left by the great philosophers will add richness and depth to your life and help you to do the right thing at the right time.

To induce you to begin your own ethical journey through our moral legacy, I have selected a few philosophers for you to consider. Short, highly condensed summaries of their major ethical thoughts are presented. As is the case with any effort to summarize, the paragraphs that follow are not meant to be complete and exhaustive expositions of each philosopher's work. The summaries present only a few of the major themes of each philosopher. Hopefully, this limited treatment of certain secular philosophers will stimulate your own more in-depth study and review.

The following summaries do not include the teachings of the great spiritual figures, prophets and leaders, since such a task is far beyond the scope of this work on ethics. There are voluminous works on spiritual teachings available elsewhere.

Protagoras of Abdera

Protagoras (490–421 B.C.) was one of the first men to declare himself a "Sophist"—one that traveled throughout the Greek world, offering instruction in return for money. Consequently, he arduously believed that virtue could be taught. His writings reveal him as an individualistic relativist. He believed that reality and truth were individual matters that depended upon a person's unique perspectives and view of the world. Thus, what was truth, reality, goodness, or right or wrong for one individual was not necessarily the truth, reality, goodness, or right or wrong for another.

Understandably, Protagoras conceived of law as a necessary agreement between members of a society to assure human survival. Protagoras noted that law represented human customs that served as restraints on the individual wills of people, guiding and defining the limits within which one could act.

Socrates

Socrates (469–399 B.C.) lived his life as a teacher. He is perhaps best remembered for his methodology of questioning and making constant inquiries into the essential nature of things and concepts. The Socratic method of teaching, characterized by the teacher's posing a barrage of questions to students is one of the modern day legacies of Socrates.

Socrates' philosophical thought included concepts such as: the importance of the soul, the need to care for

the soul, introspection, self-examination, happiness, wisdom, self-control and self-mastery.

Socrates conceived of the soul as intelligence and
character. He sought to improve the soul and believed
that virtue and excellence were the critical elements. He
believed that piety, justice, courage, prudence, beauty
and health were virtues that one ought to develop and
demonstrate in one's life.

Socrates taught that self-mastery and self-control were
crucial if one desired to live a virtuous life. He recognized
the adverse effects of human passion and impulses on the
soul. He urged people to develop a strong inner life of
contemplation, to reason, to bring to bear their intellect
and to practice discipline as a means of understanding
oneself, acquiring wisdom and overcoming human
desires. Socrates taught that self-control allows freedom
from human passions, and that the lack of self-mastery
and self-control causes one to remain a slave to human
impulses.

Socrates also believed that a person should not engage
in conduct based upon a personal belief of its goodness
without also understanding the underlying basis for that
belief.

Socrates is believed to have said that if you want to
know a man's morals, look at his personal conduct, for it
is in such behavior that a man's morals are evident.

Socrates was charged with sedition and conspiracy. His critics feared him and believed that his teachings were corrupting the youth of the state. Socrates defended himself in his trial, but was convicted and sentenced to death. Socrates' friends were prepared to help him escape and avoid the death penalty. Socrates, however, declined the offer of help, and in a grand gesture of self-mastery and control, complied with the authorities by consuming the deadly hemlock cocktail that brought about his death.

Plato

Plato (429–347 B.C.) was a student of Socrates and a prolific writer. He echoed Socrates' focus on the soul. He believed it is of great importance to educate the soul, understand it and control it through the exercise of reason. He believed the soul to be capable of self-direction toward goodness.

Plato conceived of the soul as consisting of three parts: the rational, spirit and desire. The rational component is capable of maintaining a balance between spirit and desire, but this task can only be accomplished through the powerful exercise of the mind.

Aristotle

Aristotle (384–322 B.C.) studied in Athens under Plato. He was summoned to be the tutor of the young thirteen-year-old Alexander the Great. When Alexander assumed the throne, Aristotle returned to Athens and established his own school.

Aristotle believed that all human conduct is guided by its ends or goals. He taught that humans have freedom of choice over their conduct. Aristotle believed that the human soul is comprised of two parts: a rational part and a non-rational part. The rational part is the place of intellectual virtue, while the non-rational is the location of appetites and of desire.

He conceived of humans as having to constantly choose between virtues and vice. According to Aristotle, vice is the result of excessive or defective activity. Virtue, on the other hand, is the mean between excess and defect. For example, courage, a virtuous state of being, is the middle ground between rashness (excess) and cowardice (defect).

Aristotle believed that the health and happiness of the soul could be achieved through training and the development of good habits. Aristotle believed that a person could become virtuous as a result of constant adherence to a pattern of good living.

He promoted adherence to the following virtues: courage, temperance, magnificence, magnanimity, proper ambition, patience, truthfulness, wittiness, friendliness, modesty and righteous indignation.

Epicurus

The philosophy and beliefs of Epicurus (341–270 B.C.) stand in contrast to those of Socrates, Plato and Aristotle. Epicurus believed that goodness and virtue were to be found in pursuing pleasure and avoiding pain. Thus, personal sensation and physical pleasure were seen as the pathways to knowledge and virtue. This view did not mean that one could engage in activities to an extreme or excess, for to do so would inevitably result in pain. Epicurus taught that one should enjoy food and delight in the pleasure it provides, but if it was consumed in excess, one would experience discomfort and pain. Epicurus' ethics required a balance of pleasure and pain, accepting some pain for subsequent pleasure and rejecting pain that led to greater discomfort.

Epicurus valued the following virtues: justice, temperance and courage.

Epictetus

Epictetus (50–125 A.D.) was born a slave, brought to Rome, educated and released upon his master's death. He became a teacher and focused on sharing concepts of how to live a virtuous life. He believed that the virtuous life consisted of knowledge, practice, truth and freedom.

Epictetus was a Stoic philosopher. His views on freedom are particularly noteworthy. He observed that freedom is not the power to do as one desires, but rather freedom is found in being able to understand one's limits—particularly what is and what is not, within one's control. By accepting one's limits and training one's desires to accept that truth, one can experience freedom. In yielding to the desire for control and things that one cannot have, one loses personal freedom.

Epictetus taught that you cannot choose the external circumstances you encounter. You can only choose how you will respond to them and how you feel about them.

Like Socrates, Plato and Aristotle, Epictetus believed in the power of the mind, rational thought and the development of good habits as a means of living a virtuous life.

It is reported that Epictetus' teacher, during an educational session, began twisting Epictetus' leg. Epictetus sat stoically and said, "You are going to break my leg." When the teacher continued and the leg was broken, Epictetus calmly remarked, "I told you so." This example of self-control epitomizes Epictetus' philosophy of Stoicism.

Marcus Aurelius

Marcus Aurelius (121–180 A.D.) was the Emperor of Rome from 161–180 A.D. He, like Epictetus, was a Stoic philosopher. He believed that a person should accept his fate, destiny, position in life and fulfill his role to the best of his ability. He believed that ill will or mistreatment could not hurt a person without that person's permission, or against that person's will or desire.

According to Marcus Aurelius, freedom is gained by accepting and responding in a rational manner, rather than in a highly agitated emotional manner. He reportedly said that the quality of one's life is dependent upon the quality of one's thoughts, echoing the belief in the power of the human mind and the need for reason and rational thought.

Nicollo Machiavelli

Nicollo Machiavelli (1469–1527 A.D.) possessed a dark and evil view of the world. His observations of his society and culture led him to believe that people are corrupt, evil and self-serving. He observed that people desire and lust, endlessly, for power, pleasure and profit. He noted that people are caught up in an intense, ruthless and competitive struggle for survival.

In light of such observations, Machiavelli believed that to survive in such an environment, one has to seek, grab, hold and exercise power for self-preservation. He did not believe in the Christian principle of self-sacrifice.

Machiavelli was probably heavily influenced by the Egoism preference.

Friedrich Nietzsche

Friedrich Nietzsche (1844–1900 A.D.) believed that the natural desire of a person is to dominate others and to reshape the world to fit one's own preferences, views and perspectives. He believed that people have unrestricted desires for conquest, passionate love and mystical ecstasy. He observed that people are engaged in a fierce struggle for power and dominance. He noted that people will readily do what they can to gain power.

He was a critic of Christianity, believing that traditional Christian values of goodness, meekness and servility created a culture that destroyed the drive for excellence, achievement and self-realization. He felt that equality, selflessness, meekness, humility, sympathy and pity were qualities of weakness.

He embraced and believed in individualistic values, such as the spirit of nobility, self-assertion, daring, creativity, passion, excellence and an affirmation of life, struggle and conquest.

Nietzsche's views identify and reveal him as one aligned with the Egoism preference.

Thomas Hobbes

Another philosopher heavily influenced by Egoism was Thomas Hobbes (1588–1679 A.D.) who felt that all human conduct arose out of an inherent need for self-preservation. He believed that the human drive for self-preservation causes a perpetual state of war in which everyone has a natural right to anything they need in order to survive. People therefore do anything in their own judgment to get out of the state of war.

Hobbes pronounced that the only way to get out of the chaos and war of survival is to have a strong government (monarchy) based on a social contract—a voluntary agreement in which everyone gives up certain rights in exchange for certain benefits and privileges.

Adam Smith

Adam Smith (1723–1790 A.D.) believed that humans are imbued by God with powerful instincts and passions that result in behaviors that, if allowed to occur, are ultimately beneficial to all. Specifically, Smith noted that humans possess an innate concern for their individual self-interest. He believed that competition among various self-interests was good and would result in the just and equitable distribution of goods and services, thereby benefiting society at large. Smith was a strong proponent of Egoism.

David Hume

The ethical thoughts of David Hume (1711–1776 A.D.) are premised upon the belief that moral convictions are based on feelings rather than reason. Hume believed that morality, or a sense of right and wrong, arises only when people react to circumstances and develop feelings of approval or disapproval. Thus, Hume advocated an emotional or intuitive model of ethics that diminished the importance of rational thought.

Clearly, Hume would encourage ethical choices based on feelings rather than absolute rules of conduct or reason. This emphasis on feelings rather than logic and rational thought distinguishes Hume from most moral philosophers.

Jean Jacques Rousseau

Jean Jacques Rousseau (1712–1778 A.D.) believed that man is by nature inherently good, but that society is the cause of all corruption and vice. He believed that each person, in his natural state, possesses a healthy self-love, which is turned into venal pride when one seeks the approval or good opinion of others in society. This state of affairs causes people to lose touch with their true inner self and results in a loss of freedom. Hence, the path to freedom is to remain true to yourself. Rousseau's beliefs form part of the basis for the Existentialism preference.

Soren Kierkegaard

Soren Kierkegaard (1813–1855 A.D.) who was born in Copenhagen is considered by many to be the father of Existentialism. Kierkegaard noted that in the process of daily living, one encounters ambiguous and uncertain life situations which force a choice between two or more incompatible alternatives. In choosing a moral path, Kierkegaard rejected the existence of objective tests of morality. He believed that moral standards can only be individually chosen, and that in the end, the choice of the individual is all that matters. Kierkegaard encouraged individualistic reflection, contemplation and freedom to choose one's own moral standards.

Jean Paul Sartre

Jean Paul Sartre (1905–1980 A.D.) noted that the moral direction of a person's life is always in question. He observed, like Kierkegaard, that we exist in situations and that these life circumstances undoubtedly affect us at a personal level. However, Sartre believed that the nature and quality of our existence in such situations is a matter of personal choice.

He believed that we possess individual freedom, which he defined as being the capacity to choose what we will be and how we will see the world. Thus the type of person we will become is dependent upon our individual consciousness and how we choose to live our life. This freedom makes us solely responsible for ourselves.

He proclaimed that we are defined by our choices and our actions. Sartre's emphasis on individual freedom and choice, aligns him with the Existentialism school of thought.

Jeremy Bentham

Jeremy Bentham (1748–1832 A.D.) believed that humans are motivated by the desire to experience pleasure and avoid pain. This, you should recognize, is the same philosophical view as Epicurus. Bentham, however, took this moral outlook one step further by proclaiming that the rightness or wrongness of an action can be judged by its tendency toward consequences that are pleasurable or painful.

Bentham believed that pleasure is the only good, and that one should undertake action that generates the greatest pleasure. When this principle is coupled with Bentham's view that our duty is to promote pleasure for everyone equally, the result is a form of Utilitarianism known as Hedonistic Utilitarianism.

John Stuart Mill

John Stuart Mill (1806–1873 A.D.) was also a Utilitarian philosopher who believed that an action is right if it brings about a greater balance of good over bad consequences. Good was defined by Mill as social welfare rather than pure pleasure, as Bentham believed. Mill pragmatically recognized that people always act to maximize their own pleasure, but he advocated that general social welfare ought to be one of the pleasures they seek.

Immanuel Kant

Immanuel Kant (1724–1804 A.D.) was a Deontological philosopher who believed that there are certain universal, absolute principles of right and wrong that transcend time and culture. Kant believed that these universal truths or duties could be discovered through reason. He believed that by following these moral absolutes, a person could achieve a virtuous life.

Kant formulated one such universal duty, which he referred to as "The Categorical Imperative." This principle was embodied in two formulations. The first formulation states that you ought to act in way that you would want others to act in similar situations. It is a version of the old rule, "Do unto others as you would have them do unto you." The second formulation states that you should treat others with human dignity and never use people as a means to an end.

Kant's Categorical Imperative represents an absolute rule of moral behavior and characterizes Kant within the Deontological tradition.

William Goodwin

William Goodwin (1756–1836 A.D.) was another philosopher who followed the Deontological tradition.

He believed that reason leads to truth and that truth leads to justice. He believed that education and environment determine one's character. Consequently, he felt that all humans have the potential to be rational and virtuous.

Goodwin proclaimed that humans have no inherent rights, only a fundamental moral duty to reveal benevolence. Although he was a proponent of reason, he did not exclude the need for affection during a moral deliberation of right and wrong. He recognized, however, that one's feelings have to be regulated during the deliberation and process of seeking benevolence and human improvement.

John Rawls

John Rawls (1921–2002) was an American philosopher whose ethics are based upon the search for fairness and justice. An action was ethical if it resulted in or promoted fairness and justice. According to Rawls, defining what is fair and what constitutes justice is extremely problematic because the one who is in the position to judge, define or determine the criteria of fairness or justice in each situation is not totally unbiased. Because each of us is aware of our circumstances in life, it is not possible for us to judge without knowing at some level how the definition of fairness or justice affects us in this life. In some way, when a person judges right or wrong from a fairness or justice perspective, self-interested bias interferes with the judgment to slant the result favorable to the one who is judging what is right and wrong.

Rawls formulated a principle he referred to as the "veil of ignorance" which was to be used when deciding right from wrong. Rawls' Veil of Ignorance requires that the person judging right from wrong must take that action which promotes fairness and justice to all, but without regard to how the consequence affects the decider of right from wrong.

The concept requires the decision maker to view the facts and circumstances from behind a veil of ignorance such that the facts can be perceived, but there is ignorance with respect to how the consequence would affect the decider of right and wrong.

An example of the application of the veil is ignorance would be in trying to determine the morality of torture of a prisoner of war in order to gain information from the prisoner. The veil of ignorance would require the actor (decision maker) to judge torture from the consequences to the prisoner (who may or may not have relevant information) and to judge torture from the perspective of the one inflicting the torture.

The veil of ignorance states that you must fashion a rule based on fairness and justice, but you must do so under the assumption that you will be immediately placed into the very situation you are deciding, but you will not know which position you will face. In our torture exercise you must judge the ethics of torture not knowing if you will be the prisoner or the person who will do the torturing, but you will face the consequences of the rule you apply. Without knowing if you will be the prisoner or the one who is to torture (i.e., you are ignorant of your actual circumstances in life) what rule about torture is fair and just? How do you now view the ethics of torture?

Baruch Spinoza

Baruch Spinoza (1632 - 1677) was a Dutch Jewish philosopher who believed that emotions and human passion required the application of reason. He believed that self-preservation was a strong determinant of human behavior and if left unchecked would have adverse consequences to others. His ethics centered around achieving a kind of balance between the strong passion of self-interest (Enlightened Egoism) and the reasonableness and rational necessity of taking care of the needs of others (Utilitarianism).

Under this dualistic approach to ethics he believed that doing good for others is in the best interests of yourself. Unlike Hobbes who argued for the creation of a strong social contract with a monarchy to mitigate self interest, Spinoza believed democracy was the ideal way to achieve the balance between self and others.

Your Favorite Philosopher

Did the foregoing summaries leave you with any impressions? Did you develop an interest, liking, or preference for any particular philosopher's beliefs? Did any of the philosophers concepts strike you as particularly meaningful? Did you develop a dislike or negative reaction to any of them?

*You must have
a defined ethical
belief system in order to be
an ethical person.*

CHAPTER 15

Step 3:
Develop an Ethical
Belief System

The third step toward achieving Ethical Virtuosity requires that you develop your own unique ethical belief system. The components of your ethical belief system should include a personal mission statement, a compilation of your core ethical principles, a statement of your core ethical values, statements concerning how you view ethics, integrity and character, a statement of your ethical mythologies, and a statement of the factors that influence your ethical beliefs.

If you have been diligent in answering the questions that have been posed in the previous chapters of this work, you should be in a position to easily review your prior efforts, make a few revisions and complete your ethical belief system.

If you have not yet done the work, now is the time. Resist your desire to read ahead. Overcome your natural hesitancy to put off answering the following questions:

- What does ethics require you to do?
- What are your ethical beliefs, principles, and criteria for deciding what is right and wrong?
- What gets in the way of your achievement of ethics, integrity and good moral character?
- What are your core values?
- How will others remember you?
- What is your purpose in life?
- What does integrity mean to you?
- What are the essential aspects of your character?
- What gets in the way of your mastery of ethical virtuosity?

CHAPTER 16

Step 4:
Practice Emotional Discipline

The fourth step toward Ethical Virtuosity involves mastering and controlling your emotions, impulses, internalizations, drives and weaknesses. In its most simplistic expression, it is recognized as self-restraint.

This dimension is important because your emotions, impulses, drives, internalizations and weaknesses can be destructive forces that impair your ability to act in an ethical manner.

Emotion has the potential to interfere with your human capacity to reason. It can hinder and obscure your ability to accurately perceive and interpret reality. It can cause ethical blindness, the inability to perceive the existence of an ethical dilemma or the unethical aspects of your own conduct. Being able to identify, manage, control and understand the range of human emotions that occur during an ethical crisis, as well as being able to understand how these emotions can negatively affect your capacity to reason, are important skills to master.

Daniel Goleman, in his best selling work, Emotional Intelligence, reminds us that there is a neurological reason why humans tend to react emotionally (experience an internalization) before responding in a rational and logical manner.

As we experience a life event, information about that occurrence is channeled through our senses and directed to the thalamus, a portion of our brain that processes and evaluates information before sending it to other parts of our brain for response. The two primary recipients of this neurological data are the amygdala and the neocortex.

The amygdala is the originator of our emotional reactions, our passions and our initial impulses. It is also the location of our emotional memories. If our amygdala is lost or destroyed, we lose our capacity for feelings and all sense of personal meaning.

When information from the thalamus is received by the amygdala, a wide range of emotional reactions become possible. The amygdala evaluates the information within the context of the current event and past experiences. It then activates, initiates, or causes a particular emotional response.

The neurological pathway from the thalamus to the amygdala is extremely short and direct. From a biological, evolutionary standpoint, this direct and quick pathway was crucial to the survival of our species, since it allowed for speedy determination of whether or not to fight or flee a dangerous situation.

The neocortex is that part of our brain that activates and controls rational and logical thought. Like the amygdala, it receives information from the thalamus and initiates a response to the neurological data it receives. The neocortex's response, however, is not an emotional response. It is a response grounded in reason and reflective judgment. Another significant difference between the amygdala and the neocortex is that the neurological pathway to the neocortex is long and circuitous. Thus the neocortex receives its information from the thalamus much later than the amygdala, whose short and direct neurological pathway allows it to respond well before the neocortex.

The neocortex sends a signal to the amygdala in an effort to bring reasoning to the amygdala's response. However, the short, direct signal from the thalamus triggers a reaction from the amygdala prior to the filtered signal that arrives from the neocortex. The result is that impulsive feelings, triggered by the amygdala, tend to override the slower-arriving rational thoughts from the neocortex.

The amygdala's initial impulses can be managed by another part of the brain known as the prefrontal lobes, located at the end of the neocortex's long, circuitous neurological pathway. Thus the moderating affect of the prefrontal lobes kicks in after the initial impulsive reaction of the amygdala. This is the natural, biological reason why humans tend to react emotionally to life occurrences before, and in many instances without, pausing, thinking and reflecting upon an effective course of action.

People who possess Ethical Virtuosity have learned how to exercise emotional discipline, control their emotional responses, delay gratification, resist the impulses initiated by the amygdala, and bring to bear the full potential of their higher-level capacity to reason in such a way that ethical and responsible conduct occurs during an ethical crisis. In essence, people who possess Ethical Virtuosity have mastered themselves and their emotions.

Does your repertoire of personal skills include the ability to exercise emotional discipline? Are you a master of your own emotions? Can you delay personal gratification and resist your emotional impulses?

Here are a few strategies to help you master this dimension of Ethical Virtuosity. First, recognize and appreciate the underlying neurological dynamics that are at work. When you seek to control your emotions, drives, internalizations, impulses and weaknesses, you are up against a formidable neurological opponent that has already triggered chemical reactions in your body. Heart rate, respiration, blood pressure and perspiration, are all elevated, most likely causing you to experience a heightened state of arousal or anxiety. You must be able to recognize the initial onset of these symptoms.

Second, you must resist the urge to take immediate responsive action. Remember, you need to give your neocortex time to receive the information and process it. Take a walk, disengage, count to ten, and buy yourself some time. Distance yourself from the immediate circumstances so that you are not forced to respond until you are emotionally and intellectually ready to do so.

Third, allow the emotional wave, internalization, impulse, or drive to dissipate or vent in a healthy manner. Exercise works great for me. Expressing your feelings in a safe place, away from the circumstances, works wonders. Find some strategy that works for you. The goal is to purge yourself as much as possible of the neurological responses that have been triggered.

Fourth, use the reflective judgment techniques outlined in the following chapter.

Fifth, find a stable, balanced, calm and trusted friend or colleague to share with and discuss your situation and options. Avoid those who are easily excitable, biased, or highly emotional. These people will only escalate what you already feel. What you need is a supportive outlet and a relaxed environment so that you can clearly think and make good decisions.

Remember that your mind has tremendous power to affect how you will respond. Give it a chance to help you.

CHAPTER 17

Step 5:
Exercise Free Will

The fifth step toward achieving Ethical Virtuosity requires that you consciously exercise your free will toward a noble and virtuous end. The extent to which you can actually exercise your free will in such a manner depends upon several factors.

First and foremost is your desire, motivation and ultimate ability to follow the other six steps toward Ethical Virtuosity. Each step along the way is critical. If you genuinely know yourself, obtain ethical knowledge, develop an ethical belief system, practice emotional discipline, demonstrate moral courage and personal accountability, and implement an individual action plan, you have a much greater chance of exercising your free will in a virtuous manner when it most counts—when you are faced with the agonizing temptations and conflicting feelings and pressures of an ethical dilemma.

The second factor is your ability to know, understand

and appreciate that you do possess free will. For some people, this realization never occurs. If you can understand what free will really means, you have a good chance of achieving Ethical Virtuosity.

The third factor is your capacity to engage in reflective judgment, a disciplined process of critical thinking. Following such a process will help you to master and control your free will.

Free Will

What is free will? What does this concept really mean? Can you define and explain it? Does it have personal significance in your life?

Free will is sometimes referred to as individual human autonomy. It refers to the notion that your heart, soul, mind, thoughts, feelings and behavior are capable of individual direction toward goodness or evil. As a human being, you are endowed with personal freedom of choice. You have the ability to choose how you feel about and how you respond to life's many demands and challenges. You have the inherent human capacity to choose the type of person you will become, the direction your life will take, how you will see the world, and how you will think and feel about your life. In essence, free will gives you the capacity to be the master of your own life.

Free will has been expressed in many different ways by

the great philosophers. St. Augustine is reported to have said that the purity of your soul cannot be lost without your consent. Plato said that the human soul is capable of self-direction toward goodness. Epictetus observed that you cannot control your external circumstances, but you can control and determine how you feel about and respond to them. Marcus Aurelius is noted to have said that your personal happiness is dependent upon the quality of your thoughts. All of these ancient expressions reflect a fundamental belief in the existence and the power of free will.

Recall the Life Paradigm outlined in Chapter 5. This simple formulation has as its core and central foundation the principle of free will and human autonomy. Do you remember the paradigm? It says, in simplistic terms, that life presents challenges, demands and dilemmas which trigger internalization's (thoughts, feelings, drives, impulses, etc.) that provide opportunities for you to choose how you will respond and define your character. When you make a choice, you exercise your free will.

Sometimes your choices are conscious, and at other times they are driven, as noted in the previous chapter, by your emotions, prejudices, biases and unconscious thoughts. The real challenge with free will is to consistently make conscious choices toward goodness and overcome the temptations, drives and impulses that get in the way.

Do you genuinely recognize and truly honor your personal human autonomy or free will in your decisions and behavior, or are you a slave to your internalizations? Do you understand and appreciate the tremendous power and potential that free will affords you in your daily life and in shaping your own future?

Exercising your free will toward goodness is much easier said than done. This is why you need to learn and practice reflective judgment techniques. Following a disciplined process of reflection before you act gives you the opportunity to express your free will and free yourself from the bondage of your personal internalizations.

Reflective Judgment

Reflective judgment refers to a disciplined process of pausing, sorting out, thinking about, contemplating and reflecting upon a situation before making a decision. It is a process of inner critical thinking and judgment which gives you the opportunity to control your internalizations and discover your authenticity by balancing your human emotions with your intellect and reason. The goal of reflective judgment is to help you consciously exercise your free will toward goodness and virtue.

Do you have a personal strategy or process that you rely upon when you are confronted with an ethical dilemma, or do you rely instead upon an undefined, sense of intuition? To what extent do you actually engage in reflective judgment? What are the specific steps that you follow? What steps should you follow to assure your exercise of free will toward goodness and virtue?

A Twelve-Step Process

To help you create your own process of reflective judgment, I offer the following twelve-step process for consideration. It is one of many avenues that can lead you to critical thinking and inner reflection. Examine it and develop your own disciplined process of reflective judgment.

1. **Manage the Initial Emotional Reaction**

   Recognize that during an ethical crisis you will experience a variety of emotional internalizations that will diminish your ability to consciously exercise your free will. Identify these emotional reactions and exercise emotional discipline as suggested in the previous chapter. Manage your emotional pathway so that you can bring to bear your intellectual capacities to reason. This means that you must reserve final judgment until the process of reflective judgment is complete.

2. **Identify the Real Ethical Issue**

   Often, decisions and judgments are made without resolving the true underlying ethical issue or dilemma. Thus, it is important to identify, characterize and articulate the specific ethical issue presented by the crisis.

3. Gather Relevant Facts

Don't assume that you have all the pertinent facts necessary to render a wise and ethical decision. Devote time to confirming the existing facts. Ask yourself what other facts you should have in order to make an informed and ethical decision. Obtain them in an expeditious manner and consider how this information affects your decision.

4. Consider the Law

Determine if there are any applicable legal requirements or authorities that govern the decision. If so, then follow and adhere to the law, unless the law itself is manifestly immoral or unjust.

5. Ask Others for Input

Don't hesitate to ask others for input or advice. It is helpful to obtain diverse opinions and perspectives. Weigh the advice carefully.

6. Consider Your Ethical Belief System

Remember that you have a primary ethical type or preference. Remember that you also are influenced by six other ethical preferences. Consider what these preferences require of you in this dilemma. Recall the guiding ethical principles that you have identified as being important to you. Determine what these principles mandate.

7. Consider Your Core Ethical Values

Recall and consider your core ethical values. Remember that your core ethical values are the ideals and beliefs that you embrace and desire to be reflected in all of your decisions. Determine how your decision can incorporate and reflect your core ethical values.

8. Make a Decision

Remember that you have free will. You have the capacity to choose your path. Make a decision grounded upon your ethical belief system and core ethical values. Make sure your decision is a conscious one that moves you closer to goodness. Bring to bear your intellect and powers of higher reasoning. Filter your emotions, but make sure that your decision is one that ultimately incorporates empathy, compassion and human dignity.

9. Let Your Decision Ripen

Do not act immediately on your decision. Give yourself the opportunity to reconsider it in the light of a new day. Sleep on your decision before finalizing it.

10. Ratify or Change Your Decision

Once you have had the opportunity to reconsider your decision, you should either ratify it or change it based upon your new thoughts and feelings. Don't hesitate to modify a prior decision if you have changed your thoughts about it.

11. Announce the Decision

If possible, tell others about your decision and your intended course of action. Going public

has a powerful way of holding you accountable
to the decision.

12. Act on the Decision

Implement your decision and behave in
accordance with the principles that guided it.

The twelve-step process is not complicated. It just
requires discipline. If you follow these steps and bring
integrity to the process, you will make more enlightened
decisions that reflect your free will and bring you closer
to Ethical Virtuosity.

Twenty Questions

An alternative technique of reflective judgment is to
develop a series of questions that you ask yourself when
confronted with an ethical decision. Here are my questions. See if they can help you gain greater ethical
insight.

1. Will my decision or conduct comply with the
   law?
2. Will my decision or conduct be consistent with
   my personal ethical belief system?
3. Will my decision or conduct reflect and
   promote my core ethical values?
4. What ethical principles or values ought to be
   the basis of my decision or conduct in this
   situation?

5. Have I considered the needs and interests of those who might be affected by my decision or conduct?

6. Will my decision be judged fair now and in the future?

7. Will I be proud of my decision or conduct?

8. What will my family think of me if they know or learn of my behavior?

9. Will my decision or conduct create value?

10. Will my decision or conduct move me closer to goodness and virtue?

11. Am I being pressured or unduly influenced by others?

12. Am I being driven by my emotions?

13. Have I filtered out my ego needs and my own self-interests?

14. Will my conduct reflect honesty, integrity and truthfulness?

15. Are there spiritual concerns or principles I ought to consider?

16. What will be the consequences of my behavior?

17. Who will benefit from my decision?

18. Who will be harmed by my conduct?

19. Will my decision or conduct permit or encourage exploitation of others or greed?

20. Are there other alternatives I should consider?

My twenty questions represent a basic starting point for critical thinking, reflective judgment and the conscious exercise of free will. What questions do you ask yourself when you are confronted with an ethical dilemma?

CHAPTER 18

Step 6:
Demonstrate Moral Courage and Personal Accountability

The sixth step toward achieving Ethical Virtuosity is the most difficult to master. It requires you to cultivate and personally demonstrate, in your daily conduct and during times of moral crisis, attitudes of moral courage and personal accountability.

Moral Courage

Moral courage means having the inner strength, conviction and fortitude to consciously exercise your free will toward goodness and virtue, regardless of the adverse consequences that may result from that decision. It means remaining true to your inner beliefs, engaging in behavior that demonstrates your principles, beliefs and values, and not wavering in the face of unpopular sentiment, criticism, or direct pressure to behave otherwise. It often requires self-sacrifice and being vulnerable to others who will seek to discredit you for your ethical views.

Moral courage is the single most important character trait for you to cultivate and possess. All of the other ethical values depend upon it. It is the foundation upon which the others rest. If you have moral courage, all of your other ethical values and virtues become real. Without it, you are left with noble but hollow platitudes.

I have observed a strange irony with respect to moral courage. Too often, a display of moral courage is frowned upon, discouraged, or heavily criticized. These negative consequences make it even more difficult for people to demonstrate personal moral courage. After all, if being a morally courageous person results not in praise, but in blame and insult, why would a reasonable person subject himself to such consequences?

Consider, for example, the executive, who upon discovering a wide-spread pattern of corporate misconduct within his organization, reports it to his superiors. When nothing is done to fix the inappropriate behavior, he goes public with the information. Ironically, the executive is not praised for his ethics, values and integrity. Instead, he is branded a "whistleblower," referred to as a "snitch," characterized as a disloyal, disgruntled employee and black-listed from the industry. These responses have been experienced by many "whistleblowers" who have sought to correct unethical practices. After all, no one likes a snitch!

At the 1998 Winter Olympic Games in Nagano, Japan, the highly favored and touted United States Men's Hockey Team, comprised of professional NHL players, failed to win a medal. The team's on-ice performance was deplorable. It was nothing, however, in comparison to the personal behavior of several team members who, after being eliminated from medal play, destroyed several rooms within the Olympic Village. The dollar cost of the damage was $3,000. Understandably, representatives from the United States Olympic Committee denounced the behavior, called for an investigation and urged those responsible to identify themselves and pay for the damage. Curiously, not one member of the Men's Hockey Team came forward. Investigations by the National Hockey League yielded no indictments of who was responsible.

The President of the United States Olympic Committee, was adamant that a proper apology be made and that those involved be appropriately disciplined. The incident was widely reported in the press. In response to growing pressure from the United States Olympic Committee, Chris Chelios, the captain of the United

States Men's Olympic Hockey team, stepped forward and, without identifying the culprits, sent a letter of apology to the Japanese along with a check for $3,000 to cover the damage.

Incredibly, as news of this development broke, the owner of the Chicago Blackhawks, Bill Wirtz, circulated to the media a letter he had written criticizing the United States Olympic Committee for their efforts in seeking the apology. In his letter, Wirtz compared the USOC leadership to Jonathan Swift, author of Gulliver's Travels, for blowing the incident out of proportion. He also compared him to Captain Queeg, the cowardly character who obsessed over stolen strawberries in the movie *The Caine Mutiny*.

I mention this incident for two reasons. First, although Chelios' apology and remittance of the $3,000 was a noble personal gesture, he lost an opportunity to demonstrate moral courage by identifying his teammates who had actually caused the damage. Second, the highly ethical stance of the Olympic Committee should have been praised as courageous, not criticized. The criticism it endured from Wirtz illustrates my point that those who take morally courageous positions are often castigated and ridiculed.

After Chelios' letter, the Executive Director of the United States Olympic Committee, was quoted as saying:

"Obviously, I'd still hope the people responsible would have the courage to say, 'Hey, we were frustrated, upset and we made a mistake.'" Odd isn't it? It really doesn't seem like such a hard thing to do. But at some inner personal level, a few professional hockey players who were given the chance to play in the Olympics can't seem to find what it takes to demonstrate the Olympic ideals of good sportsmanship. In this instance, moral courage was totally lacking in these individuals.

To be morally courageous requires great inner conviction that many are unable to find. These people will never achieve Ethical Virtuosity. Those, however, who consistently demonstrate moral courage will achieve ethical virtuosity.

I was recently told a story about a police captain who one night received a phone call from the jail's evening shift commander. It seems the captain's 17-year-old son had been drinking and had been picked up by an officer for public intoxication. The youth was being detained at the jail, and the shift commander wanted to know what to do with the captain's son.

The captain loved his son deeply. This was the first instance of any trouble with the star student and athlete who was destined to go on to college on a scholarship. The captain knew that the conditions at the jail were harsh. He dreaded the thought of his beloved son being incarcerated, particularly when the other inmates would be aware that the boy was the son of a police captain. The jail's shift commander was a good personal friend and would have done whatever the captain wanted. The captain was tempted by his emotions to ask that his son be released. After agonizing over it for several minutes, however, the captain asked the jail commander what would happen if his son had not been the child of a police captain. The jail commander told him the boy would not be released, but would be detained and booked. The captain, with great pain in his heart, thanked the jail commander for his call, and told him to treat his son just like any other youth charged with the same crime.

Although some people have told me they felt the captain's decision was wrong—and I suspect most loving fathers—know at a deep personal level that this is what moral courage is all about.

Don't you agree that we need a lot more people like the police captain and fewer people like the irresponsible players on the 1998 Olympic Men's Hockey Team?

Personal Accountability

In addition to moral courage, the sixth step toward Ethical Virtuosity requires that you hold yourself personally accountable for your own actions. We seem to be living in a time when personal accountability is overshadowed by attempts to evade the consequences of our decisions and behavior.

Lawsuits are burdening our courts because people are breaching their contracts, making defective products that maim people, engaging in deceptive and fraudulent business practices, and generally refusing to act in a responsible manner. The days of a verbal promise and a handshake have been replaced by voluminous pages of detailed contractual language specifying contingencies for every possibility. It seems rare to encounter a person whose word is sufficient and reliable.

I am reminded of a story told to me years ago by a law professor who was trying to explain the true nature of what it means to be a lawyer in our judicial system. The story goes like this.

Mrs. Jones owned a goat. It was a friendly goat, but like many goats, it preferred a variety of foods. Normally, Mrs. Jones kept her goat tied securely to a fence post so it would not wander away and menace the neighbors.

Mrs. Smith lived next door to Mrs. Jones. Smith loved flowers and spent most of her spring and summer months cultivating beautiful flowers, which were prized and valued by many of her friends. During the last several years, she had even begun to make money off the sale of her flowers. Flowers, it seems, were Mrs. Smith's reason for existence.

One day, Jones' goat gnawed through the rope securing her to the fence post. The goat made its way to Smith's treasured flower garden and proceeded to dine to its heart's content, virtually destroying all of the seedlings, sprouts and flowers Smith had so diligently planted and cared for.

When Smith discovered the goat standing in her garden with a few flowers hanging from its mouth, she became unraveled and attacked the goat with her fists. The goat managed a quick bite to Smith's left leg. Enraged, Smith picked up a hoe and chased the goat out of her garden. Fortunately for the goat, it managed to escape Smith's wrath. Unfortunately for Smith, however, when she returned to her garden she slipped on a hose and broke her hip, requiring a total hip replacement. After her surgery, Smith developed a serious life-threatening staph infection that resulted in the amputation of her left leg.

To say the least, Smith was a bit peeved and she sued Jones and her own surgeon. She claimed Jones was responsible for her lost flowers, her amputated left leg from the goat bite, her hip replacement, emotional distress, and pain and suffering. She claimed the surgeon was negligent in not properly treating the staph infection.

Jones denied all responsibility for Smith's condition.

First, Jones claimed that her goat was the victim of a mistaken identity, and that it was not her goat that ate Smith's flowers. Secondly, Jones alleged that if it was her goat that did the dastardly deed, her goat was not guilty by reason of insanity—caused by the traumatic separation it suffered when it was prematurely taken from its parents. Third, if it was her goat, her goat had been lost for several days, seeking refuge in another part of the city in order to escape the maniacal ravings of Smith. Fourth, if it was her goat, it had become ill as a result of eating the toxic and hazardous flowers Smith cultivated, suffering miserably and causing Jones to incur substantial veterinary fees. Fifth, Jones herself was suffering great emotional distress from the absence of her goat and its illness. Sixth, Jones contended that any injuries Smith may have suffered, were caused to herself by boxing with the goat and not seeing her own garden hose. Not only did Jones deny liability, but she countersued Smith for her goat's losses and her own emotional distress.

The surgeon denied any liability to Smith, saying it was the goat bite on Smith's leg that caused the staph infection, and that he was a surgeon, not a bacteriologist. When Smith's HMO failed to pay for the amputation, saying it had not been approved in advance, the surgeon sued Smith for payment.

Smith in turn sued her HMO for breach of contract.

The HMO went bankrupt and did not bother to file a response.

Although this story is humorous, it does illustrate my point that we as a society have lost our sense of personal accountability. Having practiced law for a good many years, I can tell you that the denials, defenses and attempts to escape personal liability that are offered up in most trials are as numerous, clever and frivolous as the defenses of Jones, the surgeon and the HMO. In fact, lawyers are handsomely rewarded and held in high esteem when they successfully get their clients off the hook.

We need to return to a sense of individual personal accountability, where we hold ourselves accountable for our actions and step up and make right that which we have caused by our erroneous decisions and conduct. This is hard to do. I know this from personal experience.

Many years ago I was travelling in southern California. I was at the end of a week-long business trip. I was tired and in a hurry to get to the airport to make my flight home. I was in a rental car and driving along a freeway that I thought would take me directly to the Los Angeles airport. I was mistaken. When I finally realized my error, I stopped and asked for directions back to the airport. The clerk at the convenience store, who barely spoke English, muttered something about turning left at the second stop light. I was running out of time. I was in an unfamiliar city. I was lost. I was running out of patience. I wanted to make that flight home.

When I came to the second stop light, I found myself in the right lane of a two-lane left turn. When I glanced down at the map to check my location, someone behind me tooted a horn. I looked up and saw the light had changed to a green arrow pointing left. I proceeded to turn left, crossed the oncoming lane of traffic and was surprised to see the ramp leading to the freeway had been barricaded by small orange traffic cones. I was already committed, since I was now in the oncoming traffic lane. It seemed odd that these orange cones had been placed in such a way that my car would easily pass through them. Before I gave it much more thought, I saw out of my peripheral vision a car in the adjacent left lane pass through the orange cones in his lane. I didn't think much and did the same. So too did all of the other cars behind me. I was about to accelerate and follow the first car to the freeway when to my surprise, a California highway patrol car came screaming down the up ramp directly toward us. To say the least, this officer was peeved. He had an attitude and I was the direct target of it. He blocked our path and commanded us to "freeze" with our hands on the steering wheels. This I did without hesitation. He came to my window and commanded me to give

him my driver's license and car registration. I immediately complied.

While he returned to his car, I had visions of disap-
pearing deep into the bowels of the California jail system.
My mind raced over my circumstances. I knew I would
miss my plane. I knew this was not my fault! After all, I
was an out-of-state business traveler, lost in an unfamiliar city, following directions given me by a foreigner. The
light had turned green with an arrow indicating the left
turn. I had an impatient driver behind me. I did not see
the orange barrier cones until I was committed and positioned in the oncoming lanes of traffic. I had no other
place to go than where I had gone. The barrier cones
were wide enough for me to pass through. I simply followed a local driver through the cones. Others had done
the same thing. I had all kinds of excuses for why I was
not responsible.

I sat there for twenty minutes while the officer spoke
to all of the other drivers behind me. Each was allowed to
go free. Finally, when he came to me, I could see he was
still agitated. I was reminded of a speech I had just given
on the need for emotional discipline and personal
accountability. As much as I wanted to tell this officer
how mistaken he was and how justified I was in my conduct, something told me this was not the right thing to
do. When he asked me why I had broken through the

barrier, I mustered all the strength I had and said in a quiet, humble voice that I was lost, I was trying to get to the airport and I had made a mistake. This was incredibly difficult to do, given my underlying emotional condition. I cringed as this officer lectured me for five minutes, telling me I had violated California law, caused a mild traffic jam and that I should be better prepared next time I came to California. This, too, was difficult to take. But something deep within me told me to simply be quiet. I had made a mistake and I needed to hold myself accountable. When the officer finished his tirade, he looked at me, shook his head and said, "Okay, since you realized your mistake, admitted it and didn't give me any lip, I'm going to let you off on this violation." I thanked him and cautiously pulled away, grateful for his benevolent exercise of discretion in my favor. I often wonder what the result would have been if I had given in to my emotions and tried to rationalize and justify my behavior. I was grateful that in this instance, I had listened to my own talk and was prepared to hold myself accountable for my own actions.

How often do you demonstrate personal accountability? To what extent do you acknowledge your errors and remedy the wrong you have caused, even when you feel that you were justified? Is personal accountability something that others believe you possess?

A friend of mine recently told me a story of a person who had obtained a new job as an office manager. This person was a bit inexperienced with the procedures of her new employer. She was responsible for submitting a variety of forms to the central corporate headquarters in order to get the payroll to the employees on time. The office manager did what she was supposed to do and the payroll checks arrived on time; that is, all but one. It seems one of the clerks had not received a check. This was not the first time this clerk had been the victim of a central headquarters payroll mistake. She told the office manager of the error and how headquarters was always screwing up the payroll.

The office manager made a few inquires and discovered that headquarters had not erred, but that she had done so when she prepared the forms. The office manager undertook the steps to submit the proper forms, but a payroll check would not arrive for ten days. She knew that no one would know that the mistake had been made by her. She thought about what she was going to say to the clerk and to the other employees who wanted to blame the headquarters for the error. She could have lied and no one would have ever known. Her image and reputation would have remained intact.

Instead, the office manager confessed to the clerk her mistake and wrote her a personal check to cover the clerk's need for funds, pending the arrival of the payroll check in ten days.

This conduct represents to me the epitome of personal accountability. The office manager was under no obligation to place her own funds at risk. She could have lied and successfully avoided all blame for the mistake. She acknowledged her error, however, and made it right. I wonder how many of us would have done the same thing. Would you have responded in such an ethical manner?

Reflections

Think back for a moment and reflect upon the concepts of moral courage and personal accountability. What do they mean to you? Are they relevant in your life? Have you missed opportunities to demonstrate moral courage and personal accountability? Do you now face a situation that calls for moral courage and personal accountability? How will you respond?

You have to make
a behavioral commitment.

CHAPTER 19

Step 7:
Develop an Action Plan

The seventh step toward Ethical Virtuosity requires
you to make a commitment. It involves developing
and following an individual plan of action. The first six
steps are really quite simple to know and understand.
The real challenge is personally following through and
demonstrating these ethical principles in your daily, personal and business conduct.

Your subordinates, co-workers, family and friends look
to you for leadership and inspiration. Are you prepared
and willing to meet this ethical challenge? Can you say
without hesitation that you will make a personal commitment to follow the seven steps to Ethical Virtuosity?

It is not too late for you to accept the ethical challenge
and make a significant statement to move yourself
toward authentic virtue and genuine goodness. If you
make a genuine commitment to achieve Ethical
Virtuosity, you will be rewarded in many ways.

The choice is uniquely and individually yours. What type of ethical legacy will you leave behind for others? Will your footprints lead them to ethics, integrity and good moral character?

Do you have the genuine desire to achieve Ethical Virtuosity? How many dimensions of Ethical Virtuosity do you now possess? Do you truly know yourself? Do you seek ethical knowledge on a regular basis? Have you developed a personal ethical belief system that is uniquely your own? Do you exercise emotional discipline when confronted with ethical dilemmas? Do you truly and consciously exercise your free will so that goodness and virtue result? Are you morally courageous and do you consistently demonstrate personal accountability?

Finally, are you willing to make a commitment and develop your individual response to the ethics challenge by developing a personal plan of action?

Part III

ORGANIZATIONAL ETHICS

12 Steps to
Achieving Ethical Virtuosity at
the Organizational Level

*Integrity involves
alignment of choices
and conduct that reflect
who you are at your inner core.*

CHAPTER 20

Organizational Ethics

How does an organizational leader promote, inspire and encourage others within an organization to do the right thing? What are the steps that lead to Ethical Virtuosity at the company level?

There are twelve simple steps that can be taken by organizational leaders to create a highly ethical corporate culture.

Step 1
Create the Desire
to Become an Ethical Organization

Someone must plant the seed for ethics within the organization. Someone must step forward and begin the process of cultivation by educating the board, management, and other influential leaders that doing the right thing at an organizational level is vital to the organization's success.

Ideally, the advocate for ethics within the organization should be the President or Chief Executive Officer—the highest leader in the organization. In some corporate structures this may be the Chairman of the Board of Directors. In a government agency, the advocate can be the head of the agency, department, division, region, or local office.

The advocate for ethics needs to have a strong personal commitment to ethics, an understanding of why ethics is important to the organization, and a willingness to tell the story and influence others.

In helping organizational leaders to cultivate a desire for an ethical corporate culture, I have found it beneficial to explain that there is a "Continuum of Organizational Morality" similar to the Hierarchy of Personal Ethics explained earlier in Chapter 5.

The Continuum of Organizational Morality consists of five types of organizational cultures: Morally Corrupt; Ethically Challenged; Legally Compliant; Ethically Striving; and Ethically Dynamic.

The Morally Corrupt organization engages in conduct that most people consider being unlawful, unethical and morally reprehensible. Oddly, this type of culture has a strong organizational ethics value system, but the ethics are grounded upon values most of us find to be reprehensible. Examples of this type of culture would include organized crime groups, international drug cartels, inner city gangs, hate groups, etc.

The Ethically Challenged organization appears at

times to be similar to the Morally Corrupt type of organization, but in reality it lacks a sense of organizing values and ethics as it develops and finds an identity. It has no ethical value system at all. It is as if the organization lacks the "corporate genetics" for ethics in its early stages of development.

The Legally Compliant organization is only concerned with obeying the law and operating within the law's narrow requirements. There is focus on compliance with the bare minimum requirements of the law without regard for the appreciation that there is a difference between being legal and being ethical.

The Ethically Striving organization knows there is a difference between law and ethics and strives to act in a manner that exceeds the bare minimum requirements of the law. The Ethically Striving organization is on the road to a higher ethical corporate culture and has developed an internal awareness of ethics, but at the corporate core the ethics are not fully developed. Form and superficiality are more characteristic of the organization's ethics culture than substance and true virtue. At times, these organizations suffer ethical failures, stumble, and in time recover and move back to an ethics focus.

The Ethically Dynamic organization places a high priority on ethics. It has no tolerance for misconduct. It rarely becomes involved in lawsuits or ethics scandals.

Executives and leaders walk the talk of ethics. They have strong corporate ideologies and solid ethical values that are known by all and followed during challenging times. Most important, others recognize the Ethically Dynamic as being an ethical organization.

The first step to developing an organizational climate that truly values ethics is to make a formal organizational commitment to become Ethically Dynamic. As mentioned previously, someone within the upper leadership levels of the organization must plant the seed. Someone must create the desire. Someone must have the personal aspiration to move the organization to Ethically Dynamic. Someone must have the vision and inspire it throughout the organization. Someone must step forward as an ethics advocate.

At a minimum, the desire to become Ethically Dynamic must be formalized by the governing body of the organization by board action or executive order. Management must be charged with the responsibility to move the organization toward Ethically Dynamic. There must be more than lip service and superficial efforts undertaken. Resources must be committed, goals must be created, strategies developed, action initiated, and executives held accounted for the movement to Ethically Dynamic.

Step 2
Conduct an Ethics Assessment

Step 2 involves an honest and forthright assessment of your organization's current ethical climate. The data from the assessment will provide the foundation for building an effective organizational ethics program.

Through a variety of techniques including personal interviews, focus groups, and a written organizational survey, you should:

- Identify your organization's vulnerability to the 60 most common forms of employee misconduct.

- Determine the common types of ethical dilemmas faced by your board, executive staff, and line personnel.

- Identify the nature and frequency of the unethical or unlawful conduct that occurs within your organization.

- Determine why such unethical or unlawful conduct occurs and identify how it can be prevented.

- Assess the effectiveness of the organizational controls or systems that are currently in place to prevent fraud, corruption, abuse and unlawful activity.

- Determine how your existing program of deterrence compares to national best practices.

The fundamental purpose of the assessment is to identify problems, issues, and concerns so that you can respond to them in an ethical manner before they become major legal or public relations nightmares.

Step 3
Establish Ethical Standards And Values

Step 3 involves establishing ethical expectations, organizational standards of behavior, and core ethical values.

The ethical expectations and standards should address the common and most frequent ethical dilemmas that occur within your organization.

The ethical values are the overall guiding principles that your board, executive staff, and line personnel are to use when exercising discretionary judgment.

Most organizations that have made a formal commitment to ethics have issued written statements of their commitment to ethics. Some organizations have issued Corporate Credos that outline the organization's overriding ethics philosophy and the reasons for its commitment to ethics. Most organizations will develop a very specific, and formalized, code of corporate conduct or business executive ethics that outlines duties and responsibilities of its employees with respect to certain commonly encountered situations. Additionally, most organizations will issue Statements of Corporate Values or

Principles which are broad aspirational guidelines employees should strive to incorporate in their choices and behaviors.

The creation of these ethical frameworks is a critical step in the process of becoming Ethically Dynamic. In essence, these ethical criteria define what is and is not acceptable behavior. The guidelines provide clarity and set the limits of what is and is not considered to be right and wrong.

Step 4
Communicate Your Ethical Standards And Values

Step 4 involves putting together an effective and persuasive communications campaign that educates your board, executive staff, and line personnel about the expectations, standards, and values the organizations has developed. The communication campaign needs to be widespread and reach out to all parts of the organization. It should include elements such as an ethics video, booklets, posters, website references, ethics newsletter, readily available copies of the Corporate Ethics Credo, Corporate Code of Conduct and Core Ethical Values of the organization.

Step 5
Ethics Training

Step 5 involves ethics training of your board, executive staff, and line personnel. Your ethics curriculum needs to be customized for each group. Your board and senior executive leadership face ethical dilemmas that require different knowledge and skills than your line personnel. They need a curriculum based on critical thinking, ethical reasoning, and practical strategies for promoting, inspiring and encouraging ethics within their respective departments.

Your ethics training also needs to cover the actual substance of your Corporate Ethics Credo, Code of Conduct and Corporate Values. Most important the training module needs to be meaningful, impactful, and not superficial. Many organizations make the mistake of thinking that ethics training should be nothing more than a one hour, self directed web- based training module. Ethics has to involve face to face training time, and must have the personal involvement of the leaders of the organization to be considered relevant and important by your line personnel.

Step 6
Measure Ethical Performance

Step 6 involves the establishment of ethical goals and targets. A basic and fundamental principle of management is that you get what you measure. Consequently, if a change in ethical attitudes and behavior is desired, you must create meaningful performance standards that are measurable so that progress toward desired ethical behaviors and attitudes can be monitored.

Step 7
Reward Ethical Achievement

Step 7 involves identifying and rewarding ethical performance by your board, senior leadership, and line personnel. People within your organization need to see that their ethical efforts are valued and rewarded. Too often in many employee cynicism develops because those who are most unethical in their performance receive rewards based solely upon performance without regard to how the performance occurred. This must be replaced with an emphasis on ethical achievement.

Step 8
Respond To Misconduct

Step 8 involves creating specific protocols and procedures for responding to allegations and instances of misconduct. Too many organizations lack a well thought out, deliberate, and planned response mechanism to allegations of unethical conduct. You need to think ahead and provide a procedurally sound and consistent organizational mechanism for responding to misconduct at all levels within the organization. Allegations of misconduct and overt unethical behavior cannot be ignored, swept aside as trivial, or diminished. Each instance must be dealt with in a manner that conveys a strong organizational commitment to ethics.

Many organizations have appointed a senior level executive to serve as the designated Ethics Officer of the organization. This person is vested with the authority to respond to allegations of unethical conduct by conducting ethics investigations under carefully delineated procedures, and making recommendations concerning organizational responses to allegations of unethical conduct. Often,

Step 9
Lead By Example

Step 9 involves having the board of directors and senior level management develop individual plans of action that will result in specific behaviors that reflect and promote ethics, integrity and good corporate conduct. It is critical that your line personnel see that the organization's leadership actually walks its ethics talk. This can only be achieved if specific behavioral plans are developed and followed.

Additionally, senior management must hold itself accountable to the same ethical standards it develops for the rest of the organization. Senior management must participate in ethics training, must behave in strict accordance with ethical standards, live the corporate credo, and exercise discretionary judgment in accordance with the corporate values and guiding principles.

Step 10
Recruit And Promote People Who Reflect Corporate Values

Step 10 involves recruiting and promoting people who believe in and reflect the corporate values. So often organizations forget to include ethics as a core competency when recruiting and promoting people. Other factors are considered, but for some reason or another, an examination of a person's ethics, integrity, and character is neglected or purposefully overlooked. This is inexcusable. If you want to build an ethical environment, you must find, recruit, promote, and retain those individuals who are naturally inclined to be ethical, and who share similar ethical values.

Step 11
Display Moral Courage

Step 11 involves having and demonstrating moral courage. This trait makes all other steps possible. Moral courage is the foundation of an organizational ethics program. There are people within organizations who do not support ethics initiatives. They argue that an ethics and compliance program is not necessary. They argue that creating an ethics program does not add anything to the bottom line. They argue that the organization is already ethical and that nothing is needed is make it better. They argue that if you start an ethics program people will think something is wrong within the organization and that a focus on ethics will be demoralizing to the morale of the employees.

These critics are ethical snipers and naysayers who are afraid to confront the reality of today's hostile legal environment, and the prevalence of unethical conduct in government, business, and the not-for profit world. Many of these critics do not see the ethical challenges that confront people day in day out in the work place. Many of them manage and lead in a reactive manner rather than proactively in an effort to prevent unethical conduct.

It takes Moral Courage to stand up to the opposition that is put up by the critics of ethics programs.

Step 12
Take Action Now

Step 12 requires that you take immediate action to create an organizational ethics program. The time is now, not later.

If you are a board member, take initiative to call for the creation of an organizational ethics program. If you are the chief executive officer or senior administrative official recommend that your organization create an ethics program. If you are a staff member or middle manager, take the time now to give your chief executive officer the information outlining the need and benefits of a strong organizational ethics program.

In addition to the steps outlined above, the other steps that can be undertaken immediately include the following:

- Appointing a senior level executive to serve as ethics officer of the organization with the specific responsibility of creating and running the organization's ethics program.

- Appointing a board level ethics committee to deal with highly sensitive organizational ethics and to serve as a global ethics oversight committee.

- Appointing an employee ethics committee to handle ethics inquiries from employees regarding what is and is not ethical conduct, and make recommendations regarding ethics training, ethical standards, and protocols.

- Creating an ethics hot line where employees can report instances of unethical conduct without fear of reprisal.

There are many ways to proceed. The most important thing for you to do is to encourage the leaders of your organization to take action.

If you do not act, who will do so?

*Ethical knowledge
and insight can help you
make better decisions,
but doing the right thing
is fundamentally a
matter of personal choice.*

Part IV

PUTTING IT ALL TOGETHER

*Ethics requires
a conscious choice
to exercise your free will
to achieve a noble
and virtuous purpose.*

CHAPTER 21

The Psychology of Ethics

Psychology is the study of the human mind, motivation, emotions, and behavior. Psychology has produced a large body of knowledge that explains how and why humans think, feel and behave the way they do.

The human mind is a complex and dynamic thing. It is more than the physical composite of the individual organic structures of the brain and its neurological pathways.

Your mind consists of your thoughts, feelings, ideas, beliefs, dreams, imaginations, and conceptions of yourself, others, and the world. Your mind is that part of you that is your conscious awareness of your physical, mental, emotional, and spiritual states of being.

Throughout this book the phrase "psychology of ethics" has been used repeatedly. Additionally, the same words make up the lead title of the book.

As used in this book, the phrase "psychology of ethics" refers to a specific body of knowledge pertaining to the inner thoughts, feelings, and processes involved in the discernment, contemplation, and ultimate determination of what is and is not ethical behavior.

The psychology of ethics presented in this book does not declare or prescribe what is right and or what is wrong. It simply describes and explains: a body of knowledge (ethical insights, principles, theoretical frameworks, and mental processes); and a way of thinking about ethics that lead to ethical virtuosity—that is, being a master at figuring out what is and is not ethical; and most important, actually doing the right thing day in and day out.

Here is a summary checklist, drawn from the substantive content of the book that lists the major aspects of the psychology of ethics—what it takes to know and do the right thing at the right time.

In essence, you need to:

- Know what ethics means to you—have a clear definition of what is ethical.
- Identify, articulate, and defend the ethical principles, values, and criteria that make up your ethical belief system.
- Understand and resolve the ethical conflicts and competing ethical demands that come from the various sources of ethics.
- Know your ethical preferences and ethical type.
- Appreciate that ethics requires more of you than the bare, minimum standards of the law.

- Base your decisions upon principles rather than situational factors.

- Understand that integrity means following your ethical beliefs consistently, regardless of the consequences.

- Know that your character is two dimensional. It consists of your ethical essence (personal moral attributes) and the personal judgments other make about you as a result of the impressions you make upon them.

- Appreciate that ethics, integrity, and good moral character are still relevant and important in today's world.

- Know the reasons why people act unethically, and most important, what has caused you to act unethically in the past.

- Follow the seven steps that lead to ethical virtuosity.

  - Develop Self Awareness
  - Know Your Ethical Beliefs
  - Seek Ethical Knowledge
  - Exercise Your Free Will Toward Goodness
  - Practice Emotional Discipline
  - Demonstrate Moral Courage and Personal Accountability
  - Take Action and Make a Personal Commitment.

- Encourage the leaders of your organization to follow the twelve steps leading to ethical virtuosity at the organizational level.

On occasion,
even good people
do stupid things.

Post Script

You have within you the seeds of greatness and the human potential for achievement.

Having a clear, strong mind, a big heart, and the courage to act on that potential is what distinguishes those who achieve greatness from those who do not.

Go forward in your life. Do so with persistence, strength, vigor, and purposefulness. Keep your eye on the horizon. Know your destination at all times. Stay on course. Overcome the obstacles you encounter.

And ... don't forget to take your brains with you!

*Authenticity
begins with knowing
your ethical type and
your ethical preferences.*

Part V

ADDITIONAL MATERIALS

*Knowing your
core values can help you
live a more virtuous life.*

Bibliography

Andrews, Kenneth R., *Ethics in Practice: Managing the Moral Corporation* (Boston: Harvard Business School Press, 1989).

Audi, Robert, ed., *The Cambridge Dictionary of Philosophy* (Cambridge: Cambridge University Press, 1995).

Badaracco, Joseph L., *Defining Moments* (Boston: Harvard Business School Press, 1989).

Badaracco, Joseph L. and Ellsworth, Richard R. *Leadership and the Quest for Integrity* (Boston: Harvard Business School Press, 1989).

Becker, Laurence, ed., *Encyclopedia of Ethics* (New York: Garland Publishing, 1992).

Casey, John L., *Ethics in the Financial Marketplace* (New York: Scudder, Stevens & Clark, 1989).

Dosick, Wayne, *The Business Bible* (New York: William Morrow, 1993).

Edwards, Paul, ed., *The Encyclopedia of Philosophy* (New York: Macmillan Company, 1967).

Goleman, Daniel, *Emotional Intelligence* (New York: Bantam Books, 1995).

Kelly, Charles M., *The Destructive Achiever: Power and Ethics in the American Corporation* (Reading, MA: Addison-Wesley, 1988).

Kidder, Rushworth M., *How Good People Make Tough Choices* (New York: William Morrow And Company, Inc., 1995).

Larimer, Louie V., *The Ethical Type Indicator* (Colorado Springs: Focused Strategies, Inc., 1996 - 2011).

MacIntyre, Alasdair, *A Short History of Ethics* (New York: Macmillan Publishing, 1966).

Madsen, P., and Shafritz, J., eds, *The Essentials of Business Ethics* (New York: Meridian, 1990).

McGreal, Ian, ed., *Great Thinkers of the Western World* (New York: HarperCollins, 1992).

Nash, Laura L., *Good Intentions Aside* (Boston: Harvard Business School Press, 1993).

Seilbert, Donald, and Proctor, William, *The Ethical Executive* (New York: Cornerstone Library, 1984).

Solomon, Robert C., and Hanson, Kristine, *It's Good Business* (New York: Atheneum, 1985).

Thomason, J., *The Ethics of Aristotle: The Nicomachean Ethics* (Great Britain: Penguin Books, 1986).

Toffler, Barbara, *Tough Choices: Managers Talk Ethics* (New York: John Wiley, 1986).

Weiss, Laurie, *What is the Emperor Wearing? Truth Telling in Business Relationships* (Boston: Butterworth-Heinemann, 1998).

The Business Roundtable Statement on Corporate Responsibility (New York: The Business Roundtable, January 1982).

Thoughts on Virtue (Chicago: Triumph Books, 1996).

*Ethical virtuosity
is the capacity
to consistently identify,
confront and resolve ethical
dilemmas in a manner
that reflects goodness.*

Focused Strategies, Inc.

Focused Strategies' mission is to help leaders promote, inspire and encourage ethics, integrity and responsible business conduct within their organizations so that the devastating consequences of internal fraud, scandal, corruption and litigation are avoided.

This mission is fulfilled by offering ethics training, ethics curriculum development, ethical leadership seminars, integrity-based leadership seminars, motivational conference keynotes and speeches on ethics and integrity, publications on ethics and integrity, ethics and compliance program planning, code of conduct assistance, ethics assessments and ethics investigations.

Ethics Training

Focused Strategies, Inc., has developed a series of highly effective, inspirational and pragmatic ethics training curriculums. These include the following:

- Integrity-Based-Leadership: 12 Steps That Promote, Inspire and Encourage Ethics, Integrity and Responsible Business Conduct

- Ethical Virtuosity: Seven Strategies to Help Leaders Do the Right Thing at the Right Time
- Understanding Your Ethical Type
- Ethical Leadership: Leadership Principles and Techniques That Work
- Identifying and Promoting Core Organizational Values
- Ethical but Effective Negotiation Techniques, Skills and Strategies

Keynote and Conference Speeches

Louie V. Larimer, President of Focused Strategies, Inc., is an accomplished motivational speaker who restores ethical visions, rekindles ethical passions and inspires integrity.

His speeches are substantive, entertaining, inspiring and laced with practical insights, substantive knowledge and down-to-earth humor. His repertoire includes:

- Leading with Integrity: 12 Ways To Promote, Inspire and Encourage Ethics, Integrity and Responsible Business Conduct
- Ethical Virtuosity: Seven Strategies to Help You Do the Right Thing at the Right Time
- Identifying Your Ethical Type: Seven Ways of Resolving Ethical Dilemmas
- Ethical Myths: Why Good People Do Stupid Things

- How to Make Ethics, Integrity and Character Meaningful and Relevant in Your Personal and Business Life

Integrity-Based Leadership

There is an urgent need for leaders of business, industry and government to promote, inspire and encourage ethical behavior and responsible decisions. This is a difficult and complex challenge that many leaders do not know how to meet. Few, if any, have had significant, relevant and practical ethics training.

When confronted with ethical or moral dilemmas, some leaders have chosen to ignore the ethical implications, while others have deliberately acted irresponsibly.

The consequences of such decisions and conduct have been devastating. They include multimillion dollar judgments, bankruptcy, outrageous attorney fees, loss of public confidence, public humiliation, decline in employee morale, loss of customer loyalty, tarnished images and destroyed careers.

It doesn't have to be that way.

The Integrity-Based Leadership Training Module was specifically designed to give leaders and managers of complex organizations the practical knowledge and skills that will enable them to foster sound ethical decisions and responsible conduct within their organizational units.

The Integrity-Based Leadership Module is suitable for first-line supervisors and above. It provides a foundation for understanding one's own ethical constitution and core ethical values. It presents a disciplined process of critical thinking and reflective judgment and introduces participants to a variety of fundamental ethical concepts and analytical principles. This results in the development of a behavior specific plan of action that will promote, inspire and encourage ethics, integrity and responsible business conduct within their departments.

The highlight of the program is the use of **The Ethical Type Indicator,** a personal assessment instrument that identifies the primary ethical preference of each participant. In addition, participants are taught how to identify their core ethical values and engage in a formalized process of reflective thought.

The Ethical Type Indicator

How do you resolve the moral and ethical dilemmas that arise in your life? Can you identify, articulate and defend the ethical principles that guide your decisions and conduct? Do you know your ethical type?

If you teach ethics, have you found a meaningful way to help your students answer the above inquiries? If you are a parent, have you found an effective tool that will help you instill conscious choices and reflective judgment skills in your children? If you are a corporate trainer, are you looking for a new, exciting and highly effective ethics training tool that will promote, inspire and encourage ethics, integrity and responsible business conduct?

The Ethical Type Indicator is a personal assessment instrument that measures the extent to which a person uses seven ethical preferences when confronted with an ethical dilemma.

The instrument consists of 42 statements or affirmations. Each statement is reflective of one of the seven different ethical preferences. The participant reads each statement and indicates the extent to which he or she agrees or disagrees with the statement.

The instrument is self-scoring and provides each participant with an individual profile of his or her ethical type and ethical preferences. The results allow and encourage individual self-discovery and self-exploration.

The instrument is also available in a format for third-party input so that participants can compare ethical type self-ratings with the perceptions of others who rate how they believe the participants resolve ethical dilemmas. This version is a powerful and insightful tool that is being used in the United States Office of Personnel Management's Western Development Leadership Center Programs.

Corporate trainers should take note that **The Ethical**

Type Indicator is best used within the context of our ***Identifying and Understanding Your Ethical Type Training Module.***

This training module outlines how to use the instrument in two-hour, half-day and full-day formats. The module is embodied in a facilitator's guide that includes specific instructions, script, overhead slide masters and interactive exercises—everything you need to conduct your own in-house training program.

Ethics Assessments

The ultimate success of any ethics and compliance program depends upon the breadth, depth and quality of the initial ethics assessment of the organization. Focused Strategies, Inc. helps leaders conduct comprehensive self-assessments of their operating environments which identify corporate business practices that unnecessarily expose the organization to liability and result in fraud, scandal, corruption and litigation. We do this in three ways.

- Personal interviews of your senior executive team to obtain perceptions concerning troublesome business practices they believe will ultimately result in some form of public embarrassment or litigation.
- Employee focus groups to solicit employee perceptions of practices that unnecessarily

expose the organization to liability and public humiliation.

- Administration of The Litigation Prevention Inventory, an assessment instrument that identifies the organization's vulnerability to 60 common forms of corporate and employee misconduct.

Ethics and Compliance Consultation

We will help you design, plan and implement an effective ethics and compliance program that meets the requirements of the United States Corporate Sentencing Guidelines.

Under this federal statute, organizations that have established effective programs of ethics and compliance are entitled to mitigation credit and the reduction of potential fines and penalties resulting from corporate and employee violations of federal law.

We have identified national bench marks and the best ethics and compliance practices which we will share with you as you plan your initiative.

The best ethical practices are organized under 17 major focus areas. We will help you to look at your current practices in relation to these national best ethics and compliance practices and then assist you in planning, developing and implementing your own unique ethics program.

Additional Information

To receive additional information, samples, or to order books, contact us.

Focused Strategies, Inc.
www.LouieLarimer.com
Louie@LouieLarimer.com
(719) 440-6410

Other Works

The author is creator of the following other publications: *Don't Poke the Gorilla in the Eye: 50 Rules for Insightful Living; The Ethical Type Indicator: A Personal Assessment Instrument; Ethical Virtuosity: Seven Steps To Help You Discover And Do The Right Thing At The Right Time; The Psychology of Personal Transformation and Change; The Life Assessment Inventory; The Life Planning Guide; 7 Strategies for Building a Successful Business; The Management Audit Matrix; The Litigation Prevention Inventory; The Integrated Leadership Training Program;* and *Becoming a 5 Star Executive: Principles, Assessment and Planning Guide*

Visit www.**LouieLarimer.com** for more information about these works..

Being
an authentic person
requires that you take
an inward journey.

About the Author

Louie V. Larimer is the Founder of Focused Strategies, Inc., the corporate entity that holds the intellectual property used in Mr. Larimer's educational programs. He is also the President/Chief Executive Officer of Midnight Sun Capital Management, LLC, a private equity company engaged in real estate acquisition, investment, development, and property management across the United States.

The author holds a bachelor's degree in psychology, a master's degree in business administration, and a juris doctorate. Mr. Larimer has taught graduate level courses in law, ethics, leadership, negotiations and conflict resolution for Regis University's School for Professional Studies, and The University of Phoenix.

He has over thirty years experience as an attorney, licensed real estate broker and corporate educator. He has spoken and presented at numerous national conferences and prominent leadership programs across the United States.

His articles have appeared in several national trade journals such as *Association Magazine, Workforce Magazine,* and *HR Focus.* He is a contributing author to *Professional Practices In Association Management,* published by The American Society of Association Executives.

He has spoken and presented at numerous national conferences and prominent leadership programs including: The National Conference On Applied Ethics; American Society For Training And Development; American Management Association; International Society For Performance Improvement; American Society of Association Executives; The United Way; The University of Denver School of Law, Graduate Tax Program; Southwestern Law Foundation Law Enforcement Ethics Conference; Amateur Athletic Union Leadership Conference; United States Racquetball Association; The National League Of Cities; United States Olympic Leadership Congress; The Council of State Governments; The United States Figure Skating Association; The Rocky Mountain Police Leadership Institute; The Medical Group Management Association; The Conference Board of Canada; Florida Department of Law Enforcement Criminal Justice Executive Leadership Program; National Association of Realtors; and The National

School Boards Association.

Mr. Larimer regularly presents leadership programs for: The United States Office of Personnel Management, Western Management Development Center; The Pacific Leadership Program; The Chinook Institute; the United States Department of Justice, National Institute of Corrections.

He provides consultation to business, government and nonprofit executives in the areas of leadership, strategy development, planning and execution, performance management, and organizational ethics and compliance.

Originally, from the island of Oahu, Hawaii, he now resides in Colorado Springs, Colorado with his family. He is an avid reader, writer, golfer, and ukulele musician.

You must know,
master and control
your emotions.

The Gift of Wisdom

If you enjoyed and gained additional insight and wisdom from your reading of The Psychology of Ethics, you might consider ordering additional copies of the book as gifts for your loved ones, friends, and colleagues.

To order:

Email: larimerg@msn.com.

Call: (719) 439-2055.

Visit: www.LouieLarimer.com